A

CHINESE AND ENGLISH

POCKET

DICTIONARY.

BY

G. C. STENT, M.N.C.B.R.A.S.,

AUTHOR OF
"CHINESE AND ENGLISH VOCABULARY," "CHINESE LYRICS,"
"CHINESE LEGENDS," "THE JADE CHAPLET,"
ETC., ETC.

SHANGHAI:
KELLY & Co., 1a, CANTON ROAD.
HONGKONG:
LANE, CRAWFORD & Co.

1874

This scarce antiquarian book is included in our special *Legacy Reprint Series.* In the interest of creating a more extensive selection of rare historical book reprints, we have chosen to reproduce this title even though it may possibly have occasional imperfections such as missing and blurred pages, missing text, poor pictures, markings, dark backgrounds and other reproduction issues beyond our control. Because this work is culturally important, we have made it available as a part of our commitment to protecting, preserving and promoting the world's literature. Thank you for your understanding.

The rapid and exhaustive sale of my "Vocabulary," coupled with the solicitations of numerous friends, will, I trust, prove a sufficient apology, if any be needed, for the publication of this little volume. The task of compilation was undertaken from a conviction of the usefulness of such a Dictionary to the foreign student of Chinese. Instead of disposing the characters in the usual order, I have arranged them, under their proper radicals, alphabetically; which on the whole, I venture to think, will be found of advantage.

G. C. S.

Shanghai, 1874.

STENT'S
CHINESE AND ENGLISH
POCKET DICTIONARY.

1
一

chang⁴	丈	a measure (10 Chinese feet = 11 ft. 9 in. English).
ch'êng²	丞	to second, to assist; an assistant.
ch'i¹	七	seven.
ch'ieh³	且	and, also, moreover, besides, further, therefore; if, should.
ch'iu¹	丘	an eminence, a mound; a name of Confucius.
ch'ou³	丑	1 to 3 o'clock A.M.; horary character; a clown, a comedian.
hsia⁴	下	below, under, down; to descend, to fall, to let fall; mean, inferior; in; to; the next.
i¹	一	a, an, one; at once; the whole; as soon as. See yi¹.
kai⁴	丐	to beg.
ping³	丙	one of the divisions of time.

A

ping⁴	並	collected together; together with; united; and, also, moreover; all; coition.
pu⁴	不	not.
sa¹	三	three.
san¹	三	three.
shang⁴	上	up, upon, on, in; to go up, to ascend; eminent, exalted, honorable; to present to a superior.
shih⁴	世	an age, a generation, thirty years; mankind.
ting¹	丁	a nail, a pin; an adult; one.
tiu¹	丟	to lose; to throw away.
yi¹	一	one. See i¹.

2
kun |

ch'uan⁴	串	to connect, to string together, strung; passing through.
chung¹	中	the middle, central; inner; in; among; half; to attain; to hit the mark.
fêng¹	丰	fine, healthy, pleasing, plump, jolly.
ya¹	丫	forked; a female slave or servant.

3
chu

chu³	主	a lord, master, sovereign; the chief, the principal; to rule, to govern.
tan¹	丹	pills; red, carnation; a red stone; the philosopher's stone.
wan²	丸	a pill; anything round.

4
p'ieh 丿

cha⁴	乍	suddenly, unexpectedly, hastily.
ch'êng⁴	乘	to ascend; to avail one's self of; Num. of sedans, &c.
chih¹	之	sign of the possessive.
chiu³	久	a long time, lasting.
fa²	乏	weary, fatigued, tired; to spoil, to injure.
'hu¹	乎	in, at, with, from, to; a note of interrogation or admiration.
kuai¹	乖	eccentric, strange, extraordinary.
nai³	乃	in, at, is, am, was, but, doubtless, certainly, forsooth; your; and.

5
yi 乙

chi¹	乩	to divine by means of sand.
ch'i³	乞	to beg, to entreat; to give.
ch'ien²	乾	heaven; the north-west. See kan¹.
chiu³	九	nine.
ju³	乳	milk; the breasts; to suck.
kan¹	乾	dry, dried up. See ch'ien².
lan⁴	亂	to confuse, to disorder; confusion, disorder; to regulate. See luan⁴.

luan⁴	亂	same as lan⁴.
yeh³	也	and, also, even, besides, likewise, still; final particle.
yi¹	乙	bent, curved; one; to mark.

6
chüeh 亅

liao³	了	final particle; finished; intelligent; fixed, determined.
shih⁴	事	affairs; actions; occupation, employment; concern; service; to serve.
yü²	予	to give, to confer, to grant; to add to; a class or sort; with; in; I, me.

7
êrh 二

chi²	亟	haste, prompt, urgently.
ching³	井	a well; 900 mu.
êrh⁴	二	two, both.
'hu⁴	互	mutual, reciprocal; to blend, blending, interlocking.
hsieh¹	些	few, some, a little of, a small quantity.
wu³	五	five.
ya³	亞	ugly; the second in order.
yü²	于	in, to, at, through, on (such a time); relating to, as to; than.
²	云	to say, to speak.

| *t'ou* 亠 | 5 | *jên* 人 |

8
t'ou 亠

*chiao*¹ 交 interchange, intercourse; to blend; to give to.

*ching*¹ 京 the capital, city where the sovereign resides.

‘*hai*⁴ 亥 horary character; 9 to 11 o'clock P.M.

‘*hêng*² 亨 successful; persevering; extensive.

*hsiang*³ 享 to receive; to enjoy; to offer up to.

*i*⁴ 亦 also, moreover, likewise, besides.

*liang*⁴ 亮 clean, bright, open.

*t'ing*² 亭 a pavilion, a dome, a portico; a watch-house; straight.

*wang*² 亡 to die, to perish; lost; forgotten; run away; destroyed; exterminated; dead.

9
jên 人

*ao*⁴ 傲 proud, haughty, uncivil.

*chai*¹ 側 oblique; to lean or lie on one side; mean, vile. See *ts'ê*⁴.

*chai*⁴ 債 to owe, to be in debt.

*chan*⁴ 佔 to grasp at, to encroach on, to usurp, to covet.

*chang*⁴ 仗 to depend on; to fight.

*ch'ang*² 償 to repay, to recompense, to revenge.

*ch'ang*¹ 倡 to guide, to lead; a leader.

chia¹	傢	household furniture, utensils.
chia¹	佳	good, excellent, fine, beautiful.
chia³	假	false, fictitious; leave of absence; to borrow.
chia⁴	價	value, the price of anything.
chiang¹	僵	to lie down, stretched out, prostrate.
ch'iao⁴	俏	handsome, pretty; as if, like.
chieh²	傑	virtue, talent; a hero or heroine; proud.
chieh⁴	介	a guest; respectable, honorable, independent.
chieh⁴	借	to borrow; to lend; to pretend; fictitious; to use metaphorically.
chien³	儉	moderate, sparing, economical, saving, niggardly.
chien⁴	健	strong, vigorous, robust, indefatigable.
chien⁴	僭	to overstep; to surpass; to assume; erroneous.
chien⁴	件	an individual article, topic, or affair; one, a, an, Num. of clothes, &c.
chih²	値	the price, worth, cost, or value of; to manage.
chih³	企	to stand erect.
ch'ih³	侈	profuse, prodigal, extravagant.
chin¹	今	now, the present time.
chin³	僅	only, hardly, barely, just about.
chin³	儘	extreme, farthest; exhausted; all, the whole.
ch'in¹	侵	to enter gradually; to invade secretly; to plunder.

ching³	儆	to warn, to caution, to forbid, to guard against.
ch'ou²	儔	a company, a party, companions.
ch'ou²	仇	to unite; a pair; hatred, animosity; proud; an enemy.
chü⁴	俱	all, the whole of; together with; both.
chüan⁴	倦	fatigue, weariness, lassitude.
chüeh²	倔	perverse, refractory, obstinate.
chün⁴	俊	great talent; excellent; good-looking, elegant, graceful.
chu⁴	住	to inhabit, to dwell; to stop, to cease.
ch'u³	儲	to collect, to accumulate, to hoard.
chuan³	傳	to transmit to, to hand down, to propagate; to publish.
chung⁴	仲	the second; a younger brother.
fa²	伐	to strike, to reduce, to cut down, to destroy.
fang³	倣	to copy, to imitate, imitation.
fên⁴	份	portion, lot, share, allotment.
fêng⁴	俸	government salaries.
fo²	佛	Buddha.
fu¹	俘	to capture in war; a prisoner, a captive.
fu²	伏	to prostrate; humble; to hide; ambush, an ambuscade; the hot season.
fu³	俯	to bend the head, to look down; to condescend.
fu⁴	傅	a tutor, an instructor; to apply, to lay on, as paint, to paint.

fu⁴	付	to give, to deliver to; to send to; to suggest.
'ho²	何	who? what? which? how? in what way? why?
'hou²	侯	the second rank of nobility, a marquis.
'hou⁴	候	time; to wait, to expect; to enquire; to protect.
'huo³	伙	household furniture.
hsi⁴	係	concern, consequences; relating to, belonging to; is, am.
hsia²	俠	chivalric, generous, disinterested.
hsiang⁴	像	like, resembling, similar; likeness; to imitate; an image.
hsien¹	仙	genii, fairies, &c.
hsin⁴	信	true, truth, trustworthy; to trust, to believe; a letter.
hsing⁴	倖	sycophantic, servile; to obtain unexpectedly, or by improper means.
hsiu¹	休	to cease, to stop; don't; good; to rest; to divorce; to repudiate; to resign.
hsiu¹	修	to direct, to regulate, to put in order, to repair, to adorn.
i¹	伊	he, she, it, they, that person or thing.
i¹	佚	peaceful, ease, rest, repose, retirement.
i²	儀	a rite, a ceremony; a rule, a pattern; correct, regular.
i²	以	to use; to order; the cause; towards, to, by; to the end that.
i³	倚	to lean against, to depend upon; to lean to one side.
i³	依	to rely on, to trust to; as, according to.
i⁴	億	100,000; an indefinite number. See yi⁴.

jên²	人	human beings, a man, *men*.
jên²	仁	humane, humanity, benevolence, charity; kernels, stones of fruit.
jên⁴	任	a trust, a post or office; to hold a post.
jêng¹	仍	again, still as before, same as formerly.
ju³	儒	learned; a scholar; a Confucianist; literati.
jung²	傭	to serve for hire; to hire.
ko⁴	個	a piece, a particle; Numerative of many things.
ku¹	估	to value; to reckon, to conjecture; the price; tax, duty.
k'uei³	傀	strange, extraordinary, monstrous; great, magnificent; a doll.
kung¹	供	to supply, to give, to offer up; to place, to arrange; to declare, to give in evidence.
lai²	來	to come, to approach; nearly; to effect.
lei³	儡	to injure, to destroy; puppets.
lei⁴	儽	idle, lazy; sickly; bending down.
li⁴	俐	clever, ingenious.
li⁴	例	laws, regulations, amendments, bye-laws; to compare; to adjust, to class, to arrange.
lia³	倆	abbreviation of *liang*; two, both.
liao²	僚	a companion, a comrade, a colleague, a fellow-officer.
ling²	伶	clever; alone; to play; to act the buffoon.
ling⁴	令	to order, to command; to warn; to cause; law, rule; period; your.
ling⁴	侌	same.

lo²	儸	superior ability; strong, active; clever.
lü³	侶	an associate, a companion, a fellow-traveller; husband and wife.
lün²	倫	species, class; kindred, relation; right, proper; constant, regular; to choose.
lung⁴	儜	ignorant, stupid, silly.
mên¹	們	plural particle.
ni³	你	you, thou.
ning⁴	佞	eloquent, specious, plausible, insinuating; quick at repartee.
o²	俄	hasty, momentary, suddenly; a sound.
ou³	偶	an image; accidental; two, a pair; to pair, to unite; an even number.
pan⁴	伴	a partner, an associate, a companion, a colleague; to accompany, to follow.
p'ang²	傍	the sides; to approach to; to lean against; left.
pao³	保	to feed, to nourish, to sustain, to protect; to guarantee, to be surety for.
pei³	俾	to enable, to cause that; to follow; to give; to benefit; to fulfil. See pi⁴.
pei⁴	佩	to respect, to esteem, to admire; to attach to the girdle; to girt; to remember.
pei⁴	倍	a multiple; to double; low, vulgar; to oppose; to act contrary to.
pei⁴	備	to prepare, to provide; ready, prepared, completed; entirely; sufficient.
pei⁴	俻	same.
pi⁴	俾	to give; to allow; to enable; to benefit; let, that. See pei³.
p'i¹	僻	unfrequented, lonely, quiet; mean, low, depraved, licentious.
pien⁴	便	convenient, expedient; cheap; accustomed to; then, thus, so; immediately. See p'ien².

p'ien¹	偏	to lean towards; inclined; partial; specially, particularly; by the side; retired.
p'ien²	便	See p'ien⁴.
po²	伯	a father's elder brother, an uncle; a senior, a superior; to control; an earl.
pu²	僕	to follow; to comply; to belong to; a servant; a disciple.
pu⁴	佈	to extend; extensive; filling the whole place.
san³	傘	an umbrella, a parasol; to cover, to shade off sun or rain.
sêng¹	僧	Buddhist priests.
su²	俗	common, vulgar, inelegant; manners, customs.
sha³	傻	idiotic, crazed, stupid.
shang³	傷	to wound, to injure, to hurt; grieved, distressed, mournful.
shên¹	伸	to extend, to stretch out; to explain, to clear up; to repeat.
shih²	什	ten; a thing, an utensil.
shih³	使	a messenger; to send; to employ, to use; to order; to cause; to answer the purpose.
shih⁴	侍	to wait upon; to be near to; to receive; to follow.
shih⁴	仕	an official; to serve; to learn; to fill an official situation.
ssŭ⁴	俟	to wait, to stay; to expect; until.
ssŭ⁴	似	resembling, like, similar to; as, as if; class, kind.
t'a¹	他	he, him, it, her, that.
tai⁴	代	a generation, an age; for, instead of, in the place of.
tan⁴	但	only, especially; but, whenever; as soon as; very.

t'ang³	儻	if, but if, should, should it be, suppose.
t'ang³	倘	same.
tao³	倒	to upset, to pour; to fall; yet, still, after a notwithstanding.
ti¹	低	low, mean; to droop, to bend or hang down.
tien⁴	佃	to plough, to cultivate; to hire.
t'ing²	停	to stop, to cease, to delay; to fix in a place.
t'ou¹	偷	to steal; by stealth, stealthily, clandestine remiss, careless; weak.
t'ung²	仝	same, the same as; with, together with; united agreeing.
tsa²	偺	I, me.
tsan¹	偺	same.
tsan³	儹	to collect together, to accumulate.
ts'an⁴	儳	to disparage; contemptuous language; irregula rapid.
ts'ang¹	倉	a granary.
tsê⁴	仄	aslant, oblique, inclined, stooping.
ts'ê⁴	側	aslant, oblique, perverted; depraved; mea vile. See chai¹.
tso³	佐	to assist; a second to; an assistant; a ministe
tso⁴	作	to do, to act, to make, to invent, to discover, begin; to arouse, to stimulate.
tso⁴	做	to do, to make; to act as, to be.
ts'u⁴	促	quick, urgent, pressing; near, close; short.
ts'ui¹	催	to press, to urge, to impel, to importune.

| jên 人 | 13 | jên 儿 |

tzŭ³	仔	careful; to sustain.
tzĭ⁴	伺	to wait upon, or for; to observe, to spy out, to examine.
wei¹	僞	false, fictitious, counterfeit, hypocritical.
wei³	偉	great, remarkable, extraordinary, surprising.
wei⁴	位	position, place, situation; a seal; a throne; right, regular, arranged.
wo¹	倭	crumpled; yielding; Japanese.
wu³	伍	five, five persons.
wu³	侮	to deceive; to injure; to despise, to ridicule, to burlesque; contempt.
wu⁴	侮	dirty; to inspect; an equal; an opponent.
yang²	佯	false, fictitious, pretended, unreal; to feign.
yang³	仰	to look up to; to trust to, to rely on; to wait upon.
yi⁴	億	one hundred thousand. See i⁴.
yu¹	優	excellent; abundant; soft, luxurious; to play, to dally, to trifle.
yu⁴	佑	to aid, to help, to protect.

10
jên 儿

chao⁴	兆	a presage, an omen; a million.
ching¹	兢	anxious, uneasy, cautious, watchful.
ch'ung¹	充	to fill, to fulfil, to act as, to play the part of.
êrh²	兒	a son, a child; a particle of sound.

hsien¹	先	before; early; to begin; in the first place.
hsiung¹	兄	an elder brother; a senior; a term of respect.
hsiung¹	兇	cruel, malevolent. Same as 凶.
k'o⁴	克	to be able, competent to; to subdue.
kuang¹	光	light, bright, shining; to illumine; to adorn; plain; naked, bare; barely, only.
mien³	免	to avoid; to dispense with; to prevent, to stop, to put off, to free from.
tou¹	兜	to raise up, to stir up, to excite; the lap.
t'u¹	兎	rabbits, hares.
tui⁴	兌	to weigh silver; to compare; to exchange.
yüan²	元	original; the origin, the beginning, the first; the head, the chief; great; black.
yün³	允	to promise, to sanction, to give assent to; sincerely, faithfully, honestly.

11
ju 入

ch'üan²	全	all, the whole of; complete, entire; to complete, to finish.
ju⁴	入	to enter; to receive.
liang³	兩	two, both; a pair, a couple; an ounce, a tael.
nei⁴	內	inside, within, internal, included in, in the midst of.

12
pa 八

ch'i²	其	he, she, it, its, his, the, that, they.

chien¹	兼	to connect; and, also, together with, additional.
chü⁴	具	arranged, prepared; placed together; to write; to present to.
hsi¹	兮	a tone of interrogation or admiration, what? how!
kung¹	公	public; just, fair, equitable; general; male; first rank of nobility, a duke.
kung⁴	共	collectively, general, all, the whole; with, together with, to include with.
liu⁴	六	six.
lu⁴	六	same.
pa¹	八	eight.
ping¹	兵	soldiers, troops, an army; weapons; to attack.
tien³	典	a rule, a law; to rule, to control; to pawn, to mortgage; a classical work.

13
chiung 冂

mao⁴	冒	blindly, rashly, heedlessly; to assume; to affirm falsely.
tsai⁴	再	again, the second time, doubled, repeated; then.
ts'ê⁴	冊	a list, an inventory, a register, a memorandum book.

14
mi ㄇ

chung³	冢	a mound, the summit of a hill; great.
jung²	冗	odds and ends; scattered; mixed; hurried.
kuan¹	冠	a cap, a crown; to cap; the head, the chief; to dress female's hair.

ming²	冥	obscure, dull, gloomy, dark; a spirit.
yüan¹	冤	to oppress, to injure; to accuse falsely; to be aggrieved.

15
ping 冫

ch'i¹	凄	intense cold; grief.
chien³	减	to break off, to lessen, to diminish, to lighten.
ching⁴	凊	cold, intense cold.
chun³	准	to approve, to authorise, to allow, to grant; to adjust, to equalize, to fix; to weigh.
ch'ung¹	冲	to boil or burst over, as water; to wash away; to fly up; to dart; young.
k'uang⁴	况	more, further, moreover, still, besides. See 況
lêng³	冷	cold, frigid, indifferent; still, clear, pure.
liang²	涼	cool, cold.
ling²	凌	ice; an icehouse; to insult, to put to shame; struck with fear.
ling³	凛	intense cold, clear and cold.
ning⁴	凝	to coagulate; to perfect, to finish; to fix, to settle.
ping¹	冰	ice.
ping¹	氷	same.
p'ing²	凭	to lean upon, to depend on; in proof of; according to; proof; at the pleasure of.
tung¹	冬	winter; the end.
tung⁴	凍	ice; cold as ice; to freeze.

16
chi 几

i^1	几	a small table.
i^2	凡	all, every; the greater part; commonly; common, vulgar; mortal.
uang²	鳳	the female of the phœnix.
g⁴	凳	a stool, a form, a bench.

17
k'an 凵

'u¹	出	to go forth or out; to produce, to beget.
in²	函	a letter; an envelope; to infold; armour.
ung¹	凶	calamity, adversity, evil, inauspicious. *misfortune*
	凸	protuberant, convex.
¹	凹	concave, hollow, indented; a pit.

18
tao 刀

¹²	刣	a despatch from a superior.
i⁴	剞	to pare even; to adjust; to mix medicine; a dose.
iao³	剿	to cut off, to destroy, to exterminate; to fatigue.
ieh²	刼	to carry off by force; to assail, to attack.
'ieh²	切	to cut, to mince; eager, urgent, important; on no account; all.

chien³	剪	scissors; to cut with scissors.
chien⁴	劍	a straight double-edged sword.
chien⁴	劍	same.
ch'ien²	前	in front of, before, in time or place; to advance.
chih⁴	制	to regulate, to direct, to rule; office.
ch'üan³	券	a deed, a bond, an agreement, a proof.
ch'u¹	初	to begin; the commencement, at first.
ch'uang⁴	創	to begin; first; to make, to invent, to found.
fên¹	分	a part, a share, one tenth; to divide, to distinguish, to separate, to halve; a candareen.
fu⁴	副	a second, an assistant; to assist; a pair, a pack, &c.
'hua²	划	a small boat; to pole a boat; a hook, a catch, a latch.
'huo¹	劉	to cut, to reap.
hsiao¹	削	to carve, to cut, to pare, to scrape.
hsing²	刑	punishment; laws.
jên⁴	刃	the edge of a knife, &c.
k'an¹	刊	to cut, to carve, to engrave.
kang¹	剛	hard, firm, stiff, unyielding; recently, just now.
ko¹	割	to cut, to cut off; to wound, to injure, to ruin.
k'o¹	刻	avaricious. See k'o⁴.
k'o⁴	刻	to cut, to engrave, to peel; ¼ of an hour. See k'o¹.

k'o⁴	尅	to overcome, to subdue; to injure, to kill.
kua¹	刮	to scrape, to pare off, to rub off.
kua³	剮	to hack to pieces, to cut the flesh from the bone.
kuei⁴	劌	to cut or break asunder.
la²	剌	to cut; to spy out. See *tz'ŭ⁴*.
li⁴	利	a sharp edge or point; acute; profit, gain, interest; to covet; to benefit.
lieh⁴	列	to separate, to distinguish; to arrange; to state in order; ranks.
liu²	劉	a weapon; to kill; to arrange; good.
p'an⁴	判	to decide, to distinguish, to judge; judgment; to unite, to join; to divide.
pao¹	剝	to flay. See *po¹*.
p'ao²	刨	to dig, to hoe, to plane, to pare off; a plane, a hoe.
p'i²	劈	to split, to tear, to rend, to divide.
pieh²	別	to part, to separate, to leave; to distinguish; another, different; don't.
p'ien⁴	片	to slice, to pare.
po¹	剝	to flay, to peel, to scrape off. See *pao¹*.
p'ou³	剖	to rip, to cut open, to split asunder.
sha⁴	刹	to nip; to pierce, to stab.
shan¹	刪	to cut out, to expunge, to cancel, to obliterate; to pare off; to revise and correct.
shêng⁴	剩	to remain; the remainder, the overplus, the surplus; not only.
shua¹	刷	a brush; to brush, to scrub, to cleanse; to put away from.

tao¹	刀	a knife, a sword.
tao⁴	到	to arrive, to go or come to; to reach or extend to.
t'i¹	剔	to cut up; to scrape off; to pick from; to reject.
t'i⁴	剃	to shave.
tiao¹	刁	dangerous, violent, ungovernable; wicked, depraved, artful.
to⁴	剁	to mince, to chop up.
tsê²	則	then, in consequence, in that case; therefore; next; cause, reason; a pattern, a law, a rule.
tz'ŭ⁴	刺	to prick, to pierce, to stab; a prickle; to punish. See la².
wan¹	剜	to cut, to pare, to carve, to engrave.
wên³	刎	to cut; to commit suicide by cutting the throat.

19
li 力

chia¹	加	to add to, to increase; additional, more.
ch'ih⁴	勅	imperial orders, decrees.
chin¹	觔	tendons, muscles; inclination; a catty.
chin⁴	勁	strong, strength; violent, overbearing.
ch'in²	勤	diligent, industrious, sedulous, laborious.
ch'üan³	券	tired, fatigued, wearied.
ch'üan⁴	勸	to advise, to exhort, to admonish, to instruct.
chüeh⁴	勵	to urge, to press upon, to compel to, to stimulate.

u⁴	助	to help; aid, help, assistance.
'ao	効	to exert one's self; efficacious; effects, proofs.
in¹	勛	merit, meritorious.
ng¹	功	merit; meritorious service; work.
,ª	勞	to give trouble to; to toil, to labour; wearied; merit; grieved; service.
	勒	to bind, to coerce, to bridle, to restrain; to engrave; a bridle.
	勵	to exert one's strength; to stimulate, to encourage, to rouse.
	力	strength, nerve, vigour, power, spirit, effort.
l⁴	劣	weak, infirm, feeble; just adequate, barely sufficient; mean, vulgar, depraved.
en³	勉	to use effort, to endeavour; to urge to, to stimulate, to persuade to.
t⁴	募	to hire; to enrol; to call upon, to invite, to beg.
³	努	to exert one's strength, effort, exertion.
!ng⁴	勝	to conquer, to win; to be superior to; to raise, to elevate; to sustain.
'h⁴	勢	influence, authority, power, strength; splendour; circumstances.
ıg⁴	動	to move, to shake, to excite, to agitate; to issue forth; to be moved; motion.
ng³	勇	brave, bold, adventurous, daring, courageous, firm, undaunted.

20
pao 勹

ı¹	勾	to hook; to entice, to inveigle; to exclude; to reject.
,¹	包	a bundle; to wrap up, to fold up, to enclose; to contain; to undertake.

shao²	勺	a spoon, a ladle; to ladle out.
wu⁴	勿	not, do not.
yün²	匀	equal, even, in even parts; to divide eq[ually]

21
pi 匕

ch'ih²	匙	a spoon; a key. See shih².
'hua⁴	化	to change; change, transformation; to to reform; to spend.
pei³	北	the north; to oppose; to retreat; perv[erse]
shih²	匙	a key; a small spoon. See chih².

22
fang 匚

chiang⁴	匠	a mechanic, an artificer, a maker of, a w[orker]
fei³	匪	not, not right; vagabonds, banditti.
hsia²	匣	a small case or box.
k'uang¹	匡	square, right; to right, to rectify; to a deliver.

23
hsi 匸

ch'ü¹	區	a store-room; to separate; small, petty
ni⁴	匿	to hide; hidden; clandestine; te absc[ond]
p'i³	匹	a piece; two, a pair; a husband or friend; to unite; to correspond to.
pien³	匾	flat; a sign board; a board or tablet.

24
shih 十

ch'ien¹	千	a thousand.
'hui⁴	卉	a general term for grass, herbs, &c.
hsieh²	協	harmony, cordiality; respect; submissive; to assist; an assistant.
nan²	南	south.
pan⁴	半	half.
pei¹	卑	low, lowly, humble; inferior, mean, base, vile.
po²	博	extensive, universal, profound; to traffic; to jest, to play.
shêng¹	升	a measure, one tenth of a *tou*, a pint; to accumulate; to advance; to ascend.
shih²	十	ten; a decimal.
tsu²	卒	lictors, soldiers; to stop; to finish; to die; hurry; sudden; a company.
wu³	午	noon, 11 to 1 o'clock; horary character.

25
pu 卜

chan⁴	占	to divine, to cast lots; to encroach; to wait.
ch'ia³	卡	a pass, a barrier; clasp of a belt. See *ka³*.
ka³	卡	a pass, a barrier, a station, a guard-house. See *ch'ia³*.
kua⁴	卦	a prognostic; divination; to divine.
pien⁴	卞	hurry, hasty, perturbed; all; a rule, a law.
pu³	卜	to divine; to conjecture, to guess.

26
chieh 卩

chi²	即	now, immediately, then; near; urgent; if.
ch'ing¹	卿	an official title; president of one of the boards; a term of respect.
chüan⁴	卷	rolled up; a scroll; a section, a book, a chapter; small.
ch'üeh⁴	却	but, nevertheless, then, therefore; really; to refuse.
ch'üeh⁴	郄	same.
hsieh⁴	卸	to unload, to put off, to unloose, to lay down, to resign.
hsü⁴	卹	to feel sorry, to pity, to compassionate.
luan³	卵	eggs of birds, testicles of animals, roes of fishes.
mao³	卯	5 to 7 A.M.; horary character; a period, time or term.
wei²	危	dangerous, imminent; danger; to endanger; to ruin.
yin⁴	印	a seal, a stamp; to seal, to stamp, to print; a type.

27
k'an 厂

chiu⁴	厩	a stable.
'hou⁴	厚	thick; weighty; great; liberal, generous, kind; intimate.
li²	厘	to subject, to regulate, to govern; name of a copper coin (cash); twins, a pair.
li⁴	厲	a grindstone; to grind, to rub; sharp, severe, stern, violent; to commence; to stimulate.
sha⁴	厦	a side room, an out-house.

i¹	厮	foragers; servants; confusion, uproar; to cut and slash.
i⁴	厭	disgust, disdain; to dislike, to hate; to reject; filled, satisfied.
an²	原	source, origin; beginning; natural; really, in fact; again; a waste, a common.

28
ssŭ, mou ム

‘ü⁴	去	to go, to go away; past, gone, former.
a¹	叄	three.
ïn¹	參	to mix, to blend; to be concerned with; ginseng. See *ts‘an¹* and *ts‘ên¹*.
an¹	參	to counsel, to advise; to join with; to impeach; to have an audience. See *shên¹* and *ts‘ên¹*.
ên¹	參	confused, irregular. *shên¹* and *ts‘an¹*.

29
yu 又

a¹	叉	to clasp the hands; a fork.
i²	及	arriving at, up to; and, at, to; to connect with.
‘ü³	取	to fetch, to bring; to take; to covet; to select; to assume.
a³	反	to turn; to return; contrary to; to act contrary to, to rebel.
ü⁴	叙	to converse, to chat.
ïn⁴	叛	to separate from, to revolt, to emigrate, to desert.
ï³	叟	an old person; term of respect for an old man; venerable, sir.
nü⁴	受	to receive, to accept, to contain; to endure, to bear, to suffer.
ï²	叔	a father's younger brother, uncle.

yu³	友	a friend, a companion, an associate; friendly, friendship.
yu⁴	又	again, further, more, moreover, still more.

30
k'ou 口

ai¹	嗳	an exclamation of pleasure, surprise, pain or anger.
ai¹	哀	compassion, pity; grief; love.
ai³	唉	an interjection; sound of reply; to sigh.
cha¹	喳	to chirrup; to reply; yes, sir.
ch'ang²	嘗	to taste.
ch'ang²	嚐	same.
ch'ang⁴	唱	to sing; to induce.
chao¹	召	an imperial summons; to call upon, to summon.
ch'ao¹	吵	to wrangle.
chên¹	嗔	to speak angrily, to scold.
chêng²	呈	a statement, a petition; to present to; to state to a superior.
chi²	唧	the noise of many voices.
chi²	吉	auspicious, fortunate, lucky, good.
ch'i¹	喊	whispers.
ch'i³	啟	to open, to explain, to inform, to instruct.
ch'i⁴	器	any utensil or instrument; ability.

*ch'i*⁴	器	same.
*chia*¹	嘉	good, excellent; to commend, to praise.
*chiao*²	嚼	to bite, to knaw, to chew; a bit, a bridle.
*chiao*⁴	叫	to call; to bid, to order; to cause; to name, *to call*.
*chiao*⁴	呌	same.
*chih*¹	吱	sound, noise.
*chih*³	啇	to stop, to desist, to be still, to rest, to stop at. See *shih*⁴.
*chih*³	只	only, but, merely, just, then.
*ch'ih*¹	吃	to eat; to drink; to bear, to suffer, to put up with.
*ch'ih*¹	喫	same.
*ch'ih*¹	㪗	to intimidate, to frighten.
*ch'in*⁴	唚	to vomit; sickening, filthy.
*chiu*¹	咎	error, fault, transgression, crime.
*chou*¹	周	to go round, to surround; to complete.
*chou*⁴	咒	to curse, to imprecate; to recite spells; to pray.
*chü*⁴	句	a sentence, a phrase, a term, a word, a line, a stop.
*chüeh*¹	噘	to purse the lips, to pout.
*chüeh*²	嗟	to sigh, to lament.
*chün*¹	君	a sovereign, a king; a virtuous man; a gentleman.
*chu*³	囑	to direct, to enjoin, to give orders or directions to.

ch'uan³	喘	to pant, to breathe short and thick.
ch'ui¹	吹	to blow, blowing.
ch'un²	唇	the lips.
fei⁴	吠	to bark, as a dog.
fên¹	吩	to talk rapidly, to sputter; to order.
fou³	否	not, if not, or not, not so.
fu¹	哺	to feed, as a child with pap, &c.
fu⁴	附	to order, to enjoin; to blow.
'ha¹	哈	to laugh loudly; to yawn; to sip; to gargle.
'hai¹	咳	an exclamation.
'han²	含	to hold in the mouth; to restrain, to repress, to check; to speak indistinctly.
'han³	喊	to vociferate, to call loudly, to call to.
'han⁴	和	with, together with, to join with, in relation with. See 'ho².
'hêng¹	哼	a sound of reply; a nasal sound; to moan, to groan.
'ho¹	喝	a shout, an angry exclamation; to drink.
'ho²	合	to close, to join, to pair, to agree, to harmonize, to suit, to answer.
'ho²	和	mild, agreeing, peaceful, complaisant, harmony. See 'han⁴.
'hou²	吼	the windpipe, the gullet, the throat.
'hou³	喉	the lowing of oxen; an angry tone; asthmatic.
'hou⁴	后	after, behind; a queen; a prince; a governor.

^{1}	呼	to call, to invoke; to address; to name.
an^4	喚	to call; to bid; to denominate, to name.
ng^3	哄	to cheat, to deceive, to beguile, to persuade.
^{1}	嘻	to laugh, to giggle, to titter.
^{1}	吸	to inspire, to inhale, to draw in, to drink, to sip.
^{1}	喜	pleasure, joy; to felicitate; to desire, to wish; to like.
t^4	唬	to intimidate, to startle; startled, frightened; anger.
t^4	嚇	same.
ing^3	嚮	to lead to, to direct to, towards, to, in the direction of.
ing^3	响	sound, noise, clamour, music; a signal, a call.
ing^4	向	towards, to, in the direction of; opposite to; time past, heretofore.
o^4	嘯	to hiss, to whistle, to roar.
n^2	啣	to hold in the mouth.
n^2	咸	all, the whole of, totally; universal, everywhere.
^{1}	噓	to blow softly; to speak in behalf of, to recommend.
an^1	喧	clamour, noise, uproar.
q^1	嚷	alteration, wrangling, noise of many voices.
	哦	noise of laughter.
^{4}	告	to tell, to inform, to announce; to order; to accuse; to pray.
q^3	哽	the gullet; a stoppage in the throat; sobbing.

ko¹	咯	to cough, to hawk. See lo⁴.
ko¹	哥	an elder brother.
ko²	鬲	to belch; unable to swallow.
ko²	呝	a sound of repetition; to belch.
ko⁴	各	each, every, various.
k'o²	咳	to cough; a cough.
k'o³	可	may, can, might, could; fit, proper, competent, worthy.
k'ou³	口	the mouth; Numerative of persons, &c.
k'ou⁴	叩	to strike, to tap, to knock, to ask; to discuss; to prostrate.
ku¹	咕	to mutter.
ku³	古	old, ancient, long ago, antiquity, remote.
k'u¹	哭	to weep, to cry loudly.
k'uei⁴	喟	to sigh, to lament.
la³	喇	loquacity, jabber, noise.
lao³	嘮	noise, clamour.
li¹	哩	a final sound.
li⁴	吏	a magistrate, a recorder, a writer, a ruler.
lieh¹	咧	sound.
lin⁴	吝	mean, niggardly, stingy, sparing; ashamed; sorry; to regret.
ling⁴	另	additional, besides, moreover, another.

lo²	囉	a tone ; prattle of a child ; troublesome.
lo⁴	咯	the noise of wrangling, disputing ; a final sound. See ko¹.
lü³	呂	the spine ; notes in music.
lu¹	嚕	speech ; to flatter ; to speak indistinctly.
lung⁴	嚨	the throat.
ma¹	嘛	a sound.
ma³	罵	to rail, to abuse, to scold ; interrogative particle, eh? what?
ming²	名	a name, a title ; to name, to designate ; fame, famous ; nominal.
ming²	鳴	cry of any bird or animal ; sound ; to sound.
ming⁴	命	fate, destiny, life, lot ; an order, a command, a decree ; will.
na¹	那	interrogative particle ; final sound ; expletive.
nang¹	嚷	to mutter, unintelligible jargon ; much talk.
nang²	囊	a purse, a bag, a sack ; to hold in a bag.
ni¹	呢	interrogative particle ; final particle ; cloth ; if ; then, when.
o¹	喔	a sound.
ou⁴	謳	to sing ; to prattle ; to be pleased ; to provoke ; to vomit.
ou⁴	喉	the windpipe, the throat, the gullet.
pa¹	叭	to open the mouth.
pa¹	吧	dumb ; wide mouthed.
p'ang³	謗	to boast ; to backbite.

p'ei¹	呸	a tone of insult, defiance or contempt; psha! pish! pooh!
p'ên⁴	噴	to puff out, to snort, to spurt, to sputter; to hoot.
p'in³	品	kind, class, grade, rank, degree; rule, limit; conduct, actions; to arrange, to classify.
sang¹	喪	to die; to destroy; to lose, to fail; to mourn, mourning.
sang³	嗓	the throat.
sê⁴	嗇	frugal, sparing, saving, niggardly; to covet.
so¹	唆	to make mischief.
sou⁴	嗽	to cough, to cleanse the mouth.
shan⁴	善	virtuous, moral, good, excellent; great; mild, gentle.
shang¹	商	a trader, a merchant; to consult, to deliberate, to devise.
shao⁴	哨	to whistle; loquacious; pointed; an outpost.
shên¹	呻	to rehearse, to recite; to sigh, to moan; to yawn; to hum.
shih³	史	history.
shih⁴	嗜	to relish, to take pleasure in, to indulge in; to desire, to lust after.
shih⁴	啻	only; to stop, to desist, to rest. See chih³.
shou⁴	售	to sell, to part with; to recompense; to respond.
shu⁴	嗽	to rinse the mouth; loquacity.
ssǔ¹	司	to manage, to direct, to rule, to control; an office; an officer.
ssǔ⁴	嗣	to succeed, succession, posterity, children, hereafter; to practise, to learn.
tai¹	呆	silly, idiotic, foolish.

t‘ai²	台	eminent, exalted; a title; sir.
tan¹	單	alone, one, single, odd, only; a bill, a permit; thin, poor.
t‘an⁴	嘆	a sigh, a long breath; to sigh, to moan.
t‘ang²	唐	dissolute; to boast; name of a dynasty.
tao¹	叨	to talk; to eat; to desire, to covet; addicted to.
t‘i²	啼	to cry, to weep, to lament; to crow; note of a bird.
t‘i⁴	嚏	to sneeze.
tiao¹	叼	to hold in the mouth.
tiao⁴	吊	1,000, 500 or 50 cash, &c.; a mace; to hang.
t‘ing¹	听	to hear, to listen; to comply, to obey; to wait. See 聽
t‘o⁴	唾	spittle; to spit. See t‘u⁴.
tu¹	嘟	to mutter.
t‘u³	吐	to spit out, to vomit; to reject; to bud, to blossom.
t‘u⁴	唾	to spit. See t‘o⁴.
t‘un¹	吞	to swallow, to bolt down; to engross.
t‘ung²	同	the same as, same, with, together with, united with, agreeing.
tsa¹	咂	to put in the mouth, to taste, to lick, to suck.
tsa²	咱	I, me.
tsai¹	哉	note of admiration, grief, doubt, surprise, praise.
tsan¹	喒	length of time; a sound.

t'sao¹	嘈	noise, clamour, disturbance.
tsui³	嘴	the mouth, the lips, a beak, a spout; a kiss.
tsui⁴	啐	to spit; to taste.
tzŭ¹	咨	despatches; to state in writing, to write; to deliberate; to sigh; to plan.
wa⁴	哇	to reach, to vomit; a sound; lascivious songs.
wei⁴	味	taste, relish, any flavour; to relish.
wei⁴	喂	to feed animals. See 餧.
wên⁴	問	to ask, to enquire, to investigate, to try judicially, to examine; to condemn.
wu¹	嗚	to sigh, to lament; alas!
wu²	吾	I, me.
wu²	吳	to talk loud, to vociferate, to clamour.
ya²	呀	an ejaculation; gaping; a sound.
ya³	啞	dumb (from birth), dumbness.
yao¹	吆	to cry or hawk goods.
yao³	咬	to bite, to knaw. See 鮫.
yeh¹	噎	to choke, to suffocate; to hiccup.
yen³	嚴	stern, severe, grave, dignified, majestic; to respect.
yen⁴	咽	the throat, the gullet; to swallow.
yen⁴	嚥	to swallow, to gulp down.
yin²	吟	to sigh, to moan; to chaunt, to recite; to hum.

yo¹	唷	an interjection.
yü⁴	喻	to manifest, to proclaim, to declare, to instruct, to explain.
yu⁴	右	the right; good, honourable; to honour; to assist.

31
wei 囗

ch'iu³	囚	to imprison, to fetter; a prison; a criminal.
ch'üan¹	圈	a pen or enclosure; a circle; to encircle; the Chinese period.
'hu²	囫	whole, complete, round, entire, in the gross.
'hui²	回	to return, to turn round; a chapter; a time, a turn.
ku⁴	固	hard, solid, stony, firm, obstinate, constant; chronic; certainly.
k'un⁴	困	fatigued, wearied, exhausted, weak; poor; to fail.
kuo²	國	a country, state or kingdom.
lün²	圇	round, complete, entire.
ssŭ⁴	四	four.
t'u²	圖	a map, plan or drawing; to plan, to scheme, to intrigue; to draw; to wish.
t'uan²	團	a ball, a lump, a mass of; round; collected together.
wei²	圍	to surround, to besiege; to guard; to limit.
yin¹	因	a cause, because of, on account of, for the sake of.
yüan²	圓	round, a circle; to make round; the whole.
yüan²	園	a garden, a courtyard, an enclosure.

32

t'u 土

ai²	埃	dust.
ch'ang²	場	an enclosure, an arena, a place for exercising, &c.
ch'ên²	塵	dust; dissipation, pleasure; carnal, worldly.
ch'êng²	城	a city wall; a walled town or city.
chi¹	基	a foundation; to found; a patrimony, a possession.
ch'iang²	牆	a wall.
chieh¹	堦	stairs, steps; a step, a degree in rank. See 階.
chien¹	堅	solid, firm, hard, stout, robust, determined.
chih²	執	to grasp, to seize, to apprehend, to retain; to manage; a manager.
ching⁴	境	a boundary or border; one's lot, place or position.
chün¹	均	equal, equality, in equal parts, impartial.
chui⁴	墜	to slide down, to descend, falling, descending.
ch'ui²	垂	to hang down, to suspend, suspended.
chung³	塚	a tomb, a grave, a hillock.
fang¹	坊	a street, a neighbourhood; to guard against.
fên²	墳	a grave, a tomb.
fên²	坟	same.

fou⁴	埠	a port, a harbour, an anchorage.
'hao²	壕	a ditch, a moat.
'ho⁴	壑	the bed of a torrent; a ditch, a pit, a pond.
'kuai⁴	壞	to injure, to spoil, to break, to ruin, to destroy.
k'an¹	堪	tolerable, able for, adequate, worthy of; to bear.
k'an³	坎	a pit; a precipice; a threshold or sill.
kang³	堽	a bank, an embankment.
k'ên³	墾	to bring waste ground into cultivation; to exert.
kêng⁴	埂	a bank, a ridge, a footpath.
k'êng¹	坑	a pit, a hole.
k'o¹	坷	uneven, rough.
kou⁴	垢	filth, dirt, mud, scurf, impurity.
k'uai⁴	塊	a bit, a piece, a portion; doltish; Num. of land, &c.
k'uei¹	圭	a kind of sceptre.
k'un¹	坤	the earth; inferior; compliance, obedience; one of the diagrams.
lei³	壘	a wall, a rampart, a fence; piled up; reiterated.
lung³	壟	a grave, a mound, a hillock.
mai²	埋	to bury, to conceal, to harbour, to lay up. See man².
man²	埋	to conceal, to harbour, to lay up. See mai².
mo⁴	墨	ink; black, obscure; to brand.

	土		31		士

	墓	a grave, a tomb, a tumulus.
	苑	ruin.
	增	an encroachment.
	積	to announce, to report, to summon, to impeach of, to recompense.
	答	to resist, to parry or, to answer, to pay back, an arrow.
	葬	to put into the grave.
	壁	a wall, a partition wall, fortress.
	延	mortar, mud, to stop or fill up, earth, marrow.
	堤	a mound, a bank, a hill.
	堡	a small citadel or fort, a station, a post, defence.
	塞	to fill, to cover, to stop, a fort, to stuff, a pass.
	塑	to make or mould an image, a clay idol.
	塲	ruined, to fall down.
	塵	pugilist, spur.
	墟	broken, ruined, a small bank broken down.
	壇	an altar, an arena.
	坐	a level plain, even, just, calm, compose, lightsome.
	堂	a hall, a temple, a mansion, a court, high, lofty, manners and respect.
	堆	a pile or pool.
	塞	an embankment, a shore, a limit, a space, design.

土   39   t'u 土

	地	the earth, the ground ; a place ; the bottom.
n⁴	墊	to fill up, to add to, to make level, to make up ; to put down; to sink.
n²	填	to add, to fill up, to make up ; to pay a debt ; entirely, completely.
	垛	a target ; to stack, to pile ; Num. of walls, &c.
	堵	to stop or close up, to shut ; to guard against ; a low wall ; settled, tranquil.
²	塗	mud ; to plaster, to smear, to daub, to defile, to efface ; a road.
³	土	earth, ground, soil ; a patrimony ; a place ; a district.
¹	堆	a heap, a pile ; to pile up, to accumulate ; a crowd ; to crowd. See tsui¹.
¹	墩	a hillock, a mound.
i⁴	在	to be, to be at, in, is in ; to dwell, to reside ; to belong to ; alive.
ıg¹	增	to add to, to increase, to augment ; to double.
	坐	to sit ; a seat ; to hold, to maintain.
i¹	堆	a pile, a group. See tui¹.
	壓	to press down, to crush, to suppress, to oppress, to humble, to subject.
²	堯	high, eminent ; a celebrated Emperor B.C. 2156.
g²	塋	a grave, a tomb.
	域	a limit, a boundary ; a state, a nation ; the world, the universe.
ın²	垣	a low wall.
ıg³	壅	to stop or close up ; to obstruct. —

shih 士　　　　40　　　　ts'ui

33
shih 士

chuang⁴　壯　strong, robust, stout, able-bodied.

'hu²　壺　a pot of any kind.

hsü⁴　壻　a daughter's husband, a son-in-law.

i¹　壹　one. See yi¹.

jên²　壬　astronomical character; north; black; wat[er]

k'o¹　壳　shell, skin, husk, &c.

k'un¹　壼　a path in the ladies' apartments in the palac[e]

shêng¹　聲　sound, noise, tone, voice; to speak; to stat[e] praise; to promulgate. See 聲.

shih⁴　士　a learned man, a scholar; a soldier; a profic[ient]

shou⁴　壽　old age, great age, long life, longevity.

yi¹　壹　one. See i¹.

34
chih 夂

None

35
ts'ui 夊

hsia⁴　夏　summer.

36
hsi 夕

ʻhuo³	夥	many, numerous; a party, a company; partners, companions.
hsi¹	夕	the evening; inclined, at right angles.
kou⁴	够	enough, sufficient. See 彀.
mêng⁴	夢	a dream; to dream; obscure.
su⁴	夙	early in the morning.
to¹	多	many, much, more, to add more; very.
wai⁴	外	outside, without, beyond; to exclude, not included in; foreign; abroad.
yeh⁴	夜	night.

37
ta 大

chi¹	奇	extraordinary, strange, surprising, wonderful, rare, odd.
ch'i⁴	契	a bond, a deed, a cheque; friends; to cut off, to terminate.
chia¹	夾	double; to nip; nippers; near to.
chiang¹	獎	to assist, to encourage, to commend, to praise.
chuang³	奘	strong, robust, stout, able-bodied.
fên⁴	奮	impetuous, vehement, precipitate; to excite, to shake.
fêng⁴	奉	to receive; to offer to; to attend to; to obey, to yield to.

| ta 大 | | 42 | ta |

fu^1	夫	a husband; a man, any working man.
hsi^1	奚	how? why? a servant, an attendant.
i^2	夷	distant, barbarian, foreign.
i^4	奕	a long time, of long continuance; chess.
$k'uei^2$	奎	between the legs; in the midst of.
$lien^2$	奩	a toilet box, a ladies' toilet.
nai^4	奈	to do something to.
$pên^1$	奔	to run, locomotion, hurry, precipitation.
$shê^1$	奢	extravagant, prodigal, wasteful; wide spread
$shih^1$	失	to lose, to miss, to fail, to neglect, to err, to take; remiss; to slip, to fall.
ta^4	大	great, large, extensive; long; fat; to enla See tai^4.
tai^4	大	large, great. See ta^4.
$t'ai^4$	太	large, great, excessive, much; very; too term of respect.
$t'ao^4$	套	an envelope, a cover, a case; a loop, a noose trap; a headstall.
$tien^4$	奠	to pour out; a libation; to offer up; to pres
$t'ien^1$	天	heaven; day; the weather; the sky; natu God.
to^2	奪	to snatch away, to grasp, to seize; to lop off criticise.
$tsou^4$	奏	any representation made to the Emperor.
$yang^1$	央	to invite, to entreat, to solicit; in the mid wide, extensive.
yao^1	夭	untimely, premature, calamitous; delicate, ten

38
nü 女

ch'ang¹	娼	a prostitute.
chên⁴	娠	to be pregnant.
chi⁴	嫉	jealousy, envy, aversion, hatred.
chi⁴	妓	singing girls; prostitutes.
ch'i¹	妻	a wife.
chia⁴	嫁	to marry (applied to the woman.)
chiao¹	嬌	delicate, tender; to bring up delicately; beautiful.
chieh³	姊	an elder sister.
chieh³	姐	same.
ch'ieh⁴	妾	a concubine.
chien¹	奸	deceitful, fraudulent, villanous, traitorous, selfish.
chien¹	姦	fornication, adultery, seduction; to intrigue, to plot.
chih²	姪	a nephew or niece.
chou²	妯	the eldest brother's wife.
ch'ü³	娶	to marry a woman.
chuang¹	妝	ladies' toilet; dressed, ornamented, rouged, made up; to pretend.
fang¹	妨	to impede, to interfere with; hindrance, obstacle, objection.
fei¹	妃	royal concubines; the heir apparent's wife.

fu⁴	婦	a wife, a house-wife, any married woman.
'hao³	好	good; very; to like; addicted to; to love suit; right, proper, fit.
'hun¹	婚	marriage; a bridegroom,
hsi¹	嬉	to play, to frolic, to ramble; handsome, pre
hsi²	媳	a wife, a married woman; a daughter-in-law.
hsien²	嫺	accomplished, genteel; skilled in; accustor to.
hsien²	嫌	aversion, dislike, prejudice, suspicion, disdai
hsing⁴	姓	family name, surname.
hsü⁴	婿	a daughter's husband, a son-in-law.
i²	姨	a wife or mother's sisters, an aunt.
ju²	如	if, as, like, according to, in accordance with.
kou²	姤	meeting, occurring, coming in contact; unior
ku¹	姑	a father's or husband's sister; a girl, a maide
lan³	婪	covetous, greedy; fraud, extortion.
li³	娌	a brother's wife.
lü²	婁	often, repeatedly; effort, exertion of streng dull, stupid.
ma¹	媽	ma, mama, mother, dame.
mei²	媒	a go-between, to arrange marriages.
mei⁴	妹	younger sisters.
mei⁴	媚	flattering, wheedling, seductive, smiling; speak to; beautiful.

miao⁴	妙	admirable, excellent, good; delicate, fine, spiritual; wonderful.
mien³	娩	to bear a child; effeminate; slow, sauntering.
mu³	姆	a schoolmistress, a governess; a matron; a midwife.
mu³	姥	same.
nai³	奶	milk; the female breast; to suckle.
nai³	嬭	same.
nĕn⁴	嫩	fresh, tender, delicate, soft, young, small, weak, fine, good.
niang²	娘	a mother, any woman.
niu¹	妞	a girl.
nü³	女	a woman, a daughter, an unmarried woman, a girl.
nu²	奴	a slave.
o²	娥	good, excellent, beautiful.
pi³	妣	a deceased mother.
pi⁴	婢	female slaves or servants.
piao³	嫖	a prostitute.
p'iao²	嫖	levity, lightness, profligacy; a prostitute.
p'in⁴	嬪	imperial concubines; handsome, beautiful.
po²	婆	a woman, an old woman, a mother.
sao³	嫂	an elder brother's wife.
shĕn³	嬸	a father's younger brother's wife; a sister-in-law.

shih³	始	the beginning; to begin, to originate; the the end that.
shu⁴	婌	a sort of female major-domo in the Im household.
shuang¹	孀	a widow; widowed.
ssŭ⁴	姒	a brother's wife.
ti³	娣	the lawful wife.
t'o³	妥	secure, safe, steady, tranquil, settled; to down.
tu⁴	妒	envious, jealous; envy, jealousy, ill-will.
tu⁴	妬	same.
tsŭ¹	姿	elegant, flattering; manner, gait, gesture riage.
wa¹	娃	a baby, babies.
wan³	婉	yielding, complaisant. See yüan³.
wang⁴	妄	incoherent; irregular; false; not existin vain.
wei¹	威	majestic, dignified; stern, severe; dignity jesty.
wei³	委	to bend down; to depute; to belong t sustain; to reject; to collect; the end.
wu³	嫵	flattering.
yao¹	妖	demons, imps, fiends, fairies, &c.; superhu
yin¹	姻	a bride; marriage.
ying¹	嬰	an infant, a baby.
yü⁴	嫗	an old woman, a mother; to nourish.
yüan³	婉	yielding, complaisant. See wan³.

39

- tzu 子

chi³	季	the seasons; the last month of each quarter; the last.
'hai²	孩	a child, children (boys or girls).
hsiao²	學	to learn, to practice; learning; to study; to imitate. See hsüeh².
hsiao⁴	孝	filial, dutiful, obedience, duty; mourning clothes.
hsüeh²	學	to study, to learn, to imitate. See hsiao².
ku¹	孤	an orphan; single, alone, solitary, destitute.
k'ung³	孔	a hole, an orifice, an aperture; Confucius.
mêng⁴	孟	the beginning of; senior; superior; large, great, Mencius.
nieh⁴	孽	crime, guilt; retribution; to waste; the offspring of guilt.
sun¹	孫	a grandchild; humble.
ts'un²	存	to preserve, to keep, to watch over, to take care of.
tzŭ¹	孳	to bear; affection for; indefatigable, diligence.
tzŭ³	子	a son, a child; seed, produce; 11 to 1; midnight; the people; a viscount.
tzŭ⁴	字	characters, written words; name, designation; mark; to cherish, to love.
ying¹	嬰	an infant, a baby.
yün⁴	孕	to be pregnant, to conceive.

40
mien 宀

an¹	安	quiet, repose, rest; safe, tranquil.
ch'a²	察	to examine, to investigate, to enquire into.
chai²	宅	a house, family or home; a grave; to fix, settle.
chai⁴	寨	an enclosure, encampment, fort or castle.
ch'ên²	宸	the Imperial apartments.
chi⁴	寄	temporarily; to entrust with; to send by.
chi⁴	寂	silent, still, lonely, quiet, repose.
chia¹	家	a house, family or home; a sect.
ch'in³	寢	to sleep, to rest; a bed chamber.
chou⁴	宙	the earth, the universe, all ages.
ch'ung³	寵	affection, love, regard, kindness; a favorite.
fu⁴	富	rich, affluent; riches; to enrich.
'hai⁴	害	to hurt, to injure; injurious, hurtful.
'han²	寒	cold; poor.
'huan⁴	宦	a government servant; an officer; a eunuch.
'hung²	宏	great, vast, wide, extensive.
hsiao¹	宵	night.
hsieh³	寫	to write, to sketch, to paint.

hsiu³	宿	a night; to rest. See *su²*.
hsüan¹	宣	to proclaim, to declare, to read loudly.
i²	宜	fit, right, proper, ought; business, affairs.
jung²	容	the countenance, aspect; to countenance, to tolerate; easy. See *yung²*.
k'o⁴	客	a guest, a visitor, a stranger, a traveller, a passenger.
k'ou⁴	寇	robbers, banditti; to pillage; a marauding excursion.
kua³	寡	few, little, seldom, rarely; single, alone; a widow; an old maid; I, me.
kuan¹	官	an officer; official; government; the senses.
k'uan¹	寬	broad, wide, roomy; liberal; forgiving; large; easy.
kuei³	宄	conspiracies; traitorous plots.
kung¹	宮	a palace; a wall; a temple; to surround.
liao²	寮	a fellow officer; a small window.
liao²	寥	empty, vacant; wide; silent, solitary.
mei⁴	寐	to close the eyes; to rest, to doze, to sleep; sleepily.
mi⁴	密	thick, close; still, silent, profound; to stop, to rest.
mo⁴	寞	silent, silence, stillness, quiet.
ning²	寧	rest, repose, tranquillity; to prefer, better to, rather.
ning²	甯	same.
pao³	寶	precious, valuable; to value.
pao³	宝	same.

su²	宿	a star, a constellation. See *hsiu³*.
sung⁴	宋	to dwell; a surname.
shên³	審	to investigate, to examine; to discriminate, to distinguish; to judge; to state.
shih²	寔	really, truly, it is so, indeed; merely, only.
shih²	實	true; solid, real; reality, facts; full.
shih⁴	室	a house, a room, apartments; a family; a wife; a grave.
shou³	守	to guard, to keep, to maintain; to protect, to defend.
ting³	定	to fix, to establish, to settle, to decide; settled, tranquil, steady.
tsai³	宰	to kill animals; to rule, to govern; a ruler, a governor.
tsung¹	宗	kind, sort; kindred, clan, family; a tablet; honourable.
wan²	完	to finish, to end; finished, ended, done, completed; entirely.
wan³	宛	yielding; bending down; crooked; as if. See *yüan³*.
yen⁴	宴	repose, leisure; a feast, a banquet; merriment.
yin²	寅	horary character; 3 to 5 P.M.; bold; strong; respectful.
yü³	宇	to cover; a room; wide, extensive; the sky, heaven.
yü⁴	寓	a lodging; to lodge, to dwell.
yüan¹	冤	to oppress, to injure; to accuse falsely; to be aggrieved.
yüan³	宛	yielding; crooked; to hang down; as if. See *wan³*.
yu⁴	宥	to excuse, to remit, to forgive, to relax; to assist; to advise.
yung²	容	the countenance; to countenance, to tolerate; easy. See *jung²*.

41
ts'un 寸

chiang¹	將	to take, to receive; to accommodate; to order; a general.
chuan¹	專	single, solely; special, in particular; to apply to solely.
fêng¹	封	to seal or close; an envelope; to proclaim; a patent.
hsin²	尋	to search, to seek; to entreat. See hsün².
hsün²	尋	to seek; to investigate; to employ; constantly; temporary. See hsin².
shê⁴	射	to shoot an arrow; to dart, to aim; to point.
shih²	射	same.
ssŭ⁴	寺	a temple, a hall, a chamber, a monastery; a eunuch.
tao⁴	導	to guide, to direct, to point out, to induce; to rectify.
tui⁴	對	opposite; an opponent; to answer, to agree, to correspond; a pair; to pair.
tsun¹	尊	honoured, honourable, eminent, noble; to honour, to respect, to venerate; you, your.
ts'un⁴	寸	an inch.
yü⁴	尉	to settle, to tranquillize; a title.

42
hsiao 小

chien¹	尖	tapering, pointed; a point, a tip or end; sharp.
hsiao³	小	small, little, trifling, petty, mean, light; I, me.
shang⁴	尚	to esteem, to value; to direct, to control; eminent; to prefer; still, even, yet, nearly, probably.

shao³	少	few, less, not much or many; slightly, to diminish; deficient; to owe; young.
ts'ao²	鄛	out of repair; coarse, rough.

43
wang 尢

chiu⁴	就	consequently; then, immediately; to coɪ to finish.
yu²	尤	extraordinary, remarkable, odd; excessiv ceedingly.

44
shih 尸

chan³	展	to open, to spread out, to expand.
chieh⁴	届	a set time; the utmost point, the extremɛ
ch'ih³	尺	the Chinese foot (14 1/10 inches English.)
chü²	居	to dwell, to reside; to sit, to rest, to stop
chü²	局	a manufactory, office, &c.; compressed; a
ch'ü¹	屈	to stoop, to submit, to crouch; bent; injɩ
i³	尾	the tail, the last, the end, the hind part wei³.
li³	履	shoes, slippers; to shoe; to tread, to walk
lü³	屢	many times, frequently, repeatedly.
ni³	尼	a nun, a Buddhist priestess; stopped, settled.
niao⁴	尿	urine; to pass urine. See sui¹.
pi⁴	屄	the vagina.

p'i⁴	屁	the posteriors.
p'ing²	屏	to cover, to screen; to reject, to put away; to keep outside.
sui¹	尿	urine; to pass urine. See *niao⁴*.
shih¹	尸	a corpse; to arrange, to set in order.
shih¹	屍	a corpse.
shih³	屎	human excrement, ordure, dung, filth.
shu³	屬	class, relation, kindred; connected; to belong to; is; absolutely; to collect.
t'i⁴	屜	a drawer; a tray; seat of a saddle.
t'u²	屠	to kill, to butcher.
ts'êng²	層	layers, stories; a step, a degree; still more intense.
wei³	尾	the tail, the hinder part, the end; small, petty. See *i³*.
wu¹	屋	a room, a house, a dwelling.
yin³	尹	a magistrate; to grasp, to rule; to introduce.

45
c'hê 屮

None

46
shan 山

an⁴	岸	a beach, bank or shore.
ch'a⁴	岔	to branch off; to miss.
ch'i²	岐	a celebrated hill; to diverge or branch off.

ch'i²	崎	hilly, rugged.
ch'ien⁴	嵌	to inlay.
ch'ü¹	嶇	rugged, hilly, mountainous.
ch'ung²	崇	lofty, eminent, noble, dignified, honourable
fêng¹	峰	the peak or point of a hill.
fêng¹	峯	same.
kang³	崗	the ridge or top of a mountain.
ling⁴	嶺	a mountain top.
pêng¹	崩	to collapse; ruined; rushing down.
shan¹	山	hills, mountains.
tao³	島	an island.
t'un²	屯	the country; a village; to exist; mi villages.
ts'ai³	崽	offspring of an animal.
wei¹	巍	high, lofty, eminent.
yo⁴	岳	a lofty mountain.

47
ch'uan 巛

ch'ao²	巢	a bird's nest; den of robbers, nest of thieve
chou¹	州	a division, a district.
ch'uan¹	川	a channel for water; mountain streams.

48

kung 工

*ch'a*¹	差	difference, mistake, error. See *ch'ai*¹ and *tz'ŭ*².
*ch'ai*¹	差	to send; the messenger sent. See *ch'a*¹ and *tz'ŭ*².
*chi'ao*³	巧	clever, artful, cunning, specious, ingenious; a genius.
*chü*⁴	巨	great, large, vast; infinite numbers, numerous.
*kung*¹	工	work; to work; a workman, a mechanic, an artificer; an officer.
*tso*³	左	the left; second to; an assistant; to verify; depraved, bad.
*tz'ŭ*²	差	irregular. See *ch'a*¹ and *ch'ai*¹.
*wu*¹	巫	a sorceress, an enchantress, a witch; magic.

49

chi 己

*chi*³	己	one's self; private, selfish.
*chih*¹	巵	a siphon; a wine vessel.
*hsiang*⁴	巷	a lane or street.
*i*³	已	finished, ended, done, past; to decline.
*pa*¹	巴	the crust which forms inside a boiler; to adhere.
*ssŭ*⁴	巳	astronomical and horary character; 9 to 11 A.M.

50
chin 巾

chang⁴	帳	curtains.
ch'ang²	常	constantly, frequently, usual, common, in the habit of.
ch'ih⁴	幟	a flag or streamer; fringed; to signalize.
chin¹	巾	a napkin; a kerchief; a head-dress.
chou²	帚	a broom; to sweep.
fan¹	幡	a long flag, a streamer.
fan²	帆	the sail of a vessel.
fu⁴	幅	a roll of cloth, silk, paper, &c.; a picture.
'huang³	幌	a curtain, a screen; a sign, (of a shop, &c.)
hsi¹	希	few, rare, seldom, unfrequent; to hope; moulting.
hsi²	席	a mat; a repast, an entertainment.
lien²	帘	a tent or booth; a flag hung up where liquors are sold.
mao⁴	帽	a hat or cap.
mu⁴	幕	a curtain or screen; a private secretary.
nu³	帑	a treasury. See t'ang³.
p'a⁴	帕	a handkerchief, a kerchief; a turban.
pang¹	帮	to help, to assist.
pang¹	幇	same.

chin 巾	57	*kan* 干

p'ei⁴ 帔 a kind of vest; a cape.

pu⁴ 布 cotton fabrics; to spread, to arrange; to infer; a spring.

shih¹ 師 skilled in; a master, a teacher, a patron, a leader, a head; a metropolis.

shih⁴ 市 a market; to trade; to encourage talent; vulgar, vicious, low.

shuai⁴ 帥 a leader, a general, a commander-in-chief.

tai⁴ 帶 a girdle, a sash; ribbon, tape; to lead, to bring; to carry on one's person; local; a neighbourhood.

t'ang³ 帑 a treasury. See *nu*³.

ti⁴ 帝 the Emperor; a monarch; a ruler; celestial virtue; the Supreme.

t'ieh³ 帖 a label; a list; a card; a petition; a copy-slip; a piece of poetry.

wei² 幃 a perfume bag; curtains.

wei² 帷 a curtain; a tent.

51

kan 干

hsing⁴ 幸 lucky, fortunate, luckily, fortunately; affection; to hope.

kan¹ 干 a shield; concern, consequence; crime, offence.

kan⁴ 幹 business; to manage, to transact, to do; ability.

nien² 年 a year, the year of a person's age.

ping⁴ 并 collected together; together with; united; and, also, moreover; all. See 並.

p'ing² 平 even, level; tranquil; to level, to adjust; to conquer; equal, fair, just.

52
yao 幺

chi³ 幾 some, several, a few; how many? about, nearly.

'huan⁴ 幻 artifice; sleight of hand; magical arts; apparitions.

yu¹ 幽 quiet, secluded, lonely, dark, hidden; imprisoned.

yu⁴ 幼 young, small, tender, of tender years; tender affection.

53
yen 广

an¹ 庵 a cottage; a Buddhist nunnery or convent.

ch'ang³ 廠 an open shed, a yard, (as a bricklayer's, carpenter's, &c.)

ch'u² 廚 a kitchen or cook-house; a slaughter-house.

chuang¹ 庄 farmhouses, homesteads; plants growing; sedate, grave. See 莊.

ch'uang² 床 a bed or couch; to rest. See 牀.

fei⁴ 廢 to annul, to lay aside, to disuse, to abandon, obsolete.

fu³ 府 a house, a palace, a store; a district; a rank; an office.

hsiang¹ 廂 side apartments.

hsiang² 庠 a school; an almshouse; a provincial graduate; to nourish.

hsü⁴ 序 order, series, arrangement, the order of precedence.

k'ang¹ 康 ease, rest, repose, comfort, tranquillity; free from ailment.

kêng¹	庚	one's age; horary character.
k'u⁴	庫	a treasury, a storehouse.
kuang³	廣	large, great, wide, extensive; to extend, to widen.
lang²	廊	apartments built east and west; passages.
lien²	廉	a corner; economical; pure, uncorrupted; to examine into.
lin³	廩	a public granary; name of an officer.
lu²	廬	a cottage, a mat hut.
miao⁴	廟	a temple.
pi⁴	庇	to cover over, to shelter; to lodge, to reside.
shu⁴	庶	a concubine; a multitude; nearly; there; in this way; so that; the whole.
ti³	底	the bottom, below; only; low, mean, menial; a rough draft. *reach to, = result in.*
tien⁴	店	a shop, an inn, a stand.
t'ing¹	廳	a court; an office; a hall, a drawing or dining room.
t'ing²	庭	a house, a hall; an office; a district.
to²	度	to think, to ponder, to guess, to surmise. See *tu⁴*.
tu⁴	度	to pass, to cross over; to ponder, to think; a degree. See *to²*.
tso⁴	座	a seat, a throne; Num. of temples, &c.
yin⁴	蔭	shade, a covering, a shelter; to screen, to shelter, to shade.
yung¹	庸	unintelligent, simple, rude, common, ordinary.

54
yin 廴

chien⁴	建	to establish, to build, to erect, to found, to raise up.
t'ing¹	廷	a hall, a court; the court; to rectify; straight, even.
yen²	延	a long time, protracted; slow, dilatory; remote, distant, extended.

55
kung 廾

kung³	廾	to bow, to salute by folding the hands.
nung⁴	弄	to make, to prepare; performing, acting, doing.
pi⁴	弊	ruined; distressed; corrupt, fraudulent; wearied, disgusted.
pien⁴	弁	military officers; a cap; a dress.

56
i 弋

i⁴	弋	an arrow, a dart; to shoot.
shih⁴	式	a fashion, a rule, a law, a pattern; to measure; to imitate; to fit; to respect.
shih⁴	弑	to murder, to assassinate; to kill a superior.

57
kung 弓

chang¹	張	a leaf, a sheet; to stretch, to spread out; to boast.

ch'iang²	强	strong, firm; overbearing, violent; good.
hsien²	弦	string of an instrument; a spring, springs; a half moon.
fu²	弗	opposed to, no, not, neither, nor, it is not so, &c.
jo⁴	弱	weak, delicate, fragile.
kung¹	弓	a bow; cover of a carriage; a land measure.
mi¹	彌	to reach to, to extend to; to spread; everywhere; to shoot an arrow.
nu³	弩	a crossbow.
pa⁴	弝	the grasp of a bow.
pêng¹	弸	full; stretched or spread out; a strong bow.
pêng¹	拼	to stretch; to draw a bow; to stretch and let go.
pi⁴	弼	to assist; to add to; to double.
t'an⁴	彈	to play on a stringed instrument; a pellet, a bullet, a ball; a bow; to draw a bow.
ti⁴	弟	a younger brother.
tiao⁴	弔	to condole, to mourn for the dead, to sympathize; to hang.
wan¹	彎	curved, bending, winding; to bend.
yin³	引	to lead, to guide; to inveigle, to seduce, to induce; to introduce.

58

ch'i 彑

'hui⁴	彙	a collection; a class or series; to class.

59
shan 彡

chang¹	彰	elegant composition; to manifest, to exhibit; brilliant.
hsing²	形	form, figure, shape, body, appearance; to shew, to describe.
p'êng²	彭	the sound of a drum.
piao¹	彪	veins, streaks; streaked; a small tiger.
ts'ai³	彩	bright colours, elegant, brilliant.
ying³	影	shadow, the shadow of.

60
ch'ih 彳

ch'ê⁴	徹	pervious, to penetrate; penetration, intelligent; passable; a road.
chêng¹	征	to go; to subjugate, to put down; to levy taxes.
chêng¹	徵	evidence; to witness, to prove, to substantiate; to collect.
ching⁴	徑	a bye-road, a footpath, a short cut; direct; the diameter.
fang³	彷	resembling, like, similar, seeming as if; uncertain.
fu²	彿	like, resembling, seeming as if.
fu²	復	to turn; again, reiterated; to reply, to retort.
'hên³	很	very, extremely. See 狠.
'hou⁴	後	after, behind, in time or place; posterity.

‘hui¹	徽	urgent, important; to understand.
hsi³	徙	to change; to remove; removed, transported.
hsü²	徐	sedate, grave, dignified, slow.
hsün²	循	to act agreeable to, to acquiesce in; to follow; to examine; to revolve.
i⁴	役	to send on government service; inferior employés. See yi⁴.
lü⁴	律	statutes, laws; to record; to distinguish; to weigh the merits of; to dress the hair.
pi²	彼	that person, place or thing; to exclude.
pien⁴	徧	everywhere, all round; to go or extend to every part; a time, a turn. See 遍.
tai⁴	待	to wait; provided against; to behave to; to treat well or ill.
tê²	得	to get, to have, to obtain; to succeed, to accomplish; able to, can. See tei³.
tê²	德	virtue, benevolence, kindness, favour; abundance; power, force.
tei³	得	must, must be, must have. See tê².
t'u²	徒	a pupil, a disciple; empty; merely; in vain, futile; to banish; rare; only; on foot; a crowd.
ts'ung²	從	to yield, to comply; to follow; by, from, through; at; with.
wang³	往	to go towards, towards, to; past and gone.
wei¹	微	trifling, minute, small; a little, rather, slightly; inferior; obscure, hidden, abstruse.
yang²	徉	to saunter, to stroll, to wander, to stray.
yi⁴	役	to send on government service; inferior employés. See i⁴.
yü⁴	御	imperial; to rule; to wait upon.

61
hsin 心

ai⁴	愛	to like, to love; to be wont, to be subj
chang⁴	悵	disappointed, vexed.
ch'êng³	懲	to repress, to curb, to caution, to c(reprimand.
chi²	急	hurried, anxious, hasty, pressed, embaɪ
chi⁴	忌	to dislike, to envy, to fear, to shun, to
ch'i¹	悽	pain, sorrow, grief, commiseration.
ch'ia⁴	恰	fortunately, opportunely, at the exact
ch'iao⁴	悄	quietly, secretly, privately; anxious, ɛ
ch'ieh⁴	怯	weak, timid, fearful, cowardly.
ch'ien¹	愆	failure, fault, crime, excess.
chih⁴	志	inclination, will, resolution, determina ographical and statistical works.
ch'ih³	恥	shame, ashamed.
ch'in²	懃	oppressed by circumstances; borne authority.
ching³	憼	to caution; sedate; anxious.
ch'ing²	情	the passions, the feelings; disposition cumstances, the facts.
ch'ing⁴	慶	excellent, beneficial, happy, blessed gratulate.
ch'o⁴	悼	pity, commiseration; to die young; an death; fear, apprehension.
ch'ou²	愁	melancholy, mournful, sorry.

ch'ou²	惆	disappointed, deceived.
chü⁴	懼	fear, apprehension, dread.
chung¹	忠	honest, loyal, faithful, upright, patriotic.
ch'ung¹	忡	grieved, sorrowful, mournful, distressed.
ên¹	恩	grace, favour, bounty, kindness, goodness.
fên⁴	忿	anger, indignation, resentment, hatred.
fên⁴	憤	grief; anger, indignation; zeal.
'han¹	憨	simple, stupid, foolish, silly, half idiotic, daft.
'hên⁴	恨	anger, resentment; dislike, hatred; to hate.
'hêng³	恆	constant, continual, of long continuance; persevering; great.
'hu¹	忽	to forget; to despise; carelessly; suddenly, unexpectedly; an atom.
'hu¹	惚	doubt, hesitation, uncertainty; small, minute.
'huai²	懷	to cherish in the bosom or breast; the bosom.
'huan⁴	患	evil, fault, calamity, misfortune, grief.
'huang¹	惶	fear, apprehension, terror, dread.
'huang²	慌	confused, hurried, unsettled, fluttered, agitated.
'huang³	恍	same.
'huang³	愰	uncertain, unsettled; to suddenly perceive.
'hui³	悔	to regret, to repent, repentance.
'hui⁴	惠	gracious, kind, obliging, liberal.

ʻhui⁴	慧	quick perception, intelligent, clever, ingenious, dexterous.
ʻhun¹	惛	confused ideas, forgetfulness, indistinct perception.
ʻhuo⁴	惑	to doubt, to suspect; to delude, to misguide.
hsi²	息	to stop, to desist, to rest; to increase; interest; to exhale.
hsi²	惜	regard, affection; to pity; to regret; sparing, saving.
hsi²	悉	to investigate; thoroughly; a thorough knowledge of, entirely; minutely; all.
hsiang³	想	to think, to consider; a thought; to hope, to expect.
hsieh⁴	懈	idle, lazy, negligent.
hsien⁴	憲	a ruler, a magistrate; to deliver laws to; well educated; experienced.
hsin¹	心	the heart, mind, motives, intentions or affections; the middle.
hsing⁴	性	disposition, temper, qualities, properties, principles; natural.
hsü¹	恤	to pity, to compassionate; to love; mournful, sorry.
hsüan²	懸	to suspend; suspense; separate.
i²	怡	to please; pleasure, joy, harmonious.
i⁴	意	to think, to consider, to reflect; to remember, to recollect.
i⁴	憶	meaning, purpose, motive, intention; ideas, thoughts, opinions.
jên³	忍	to bear patiently, to endure; fortitude, patience; to forbear.
kʻai³	慨	generous, magnanimous, liberal.
kan²	感	grateful; to move, to influence, to affect.
kʻên³	懇	to beg, to entreat, to request earnestly; sincerely.

i⁴	怪	strange, singular, monstrous, unnatural, super-human.
u⁴	快	fast, quickly, soon, shortly; sharp; cheerfulness, joy, happiness.
n¹	懽	joy, pleasure, delight, satisfaction.
n⁴	慣	accustomed to, practised in, used to.
i⁴	愧	shame, ashamed, abashed.
g¹	恭	courteous, sedate, serious, respectful, reverential.
ŋ³	恐	fear, apprehension, alarm, affright; suspicion; to imagine; to dread.
	懶	idle, lazy, indolent, negligent, remiss.
⁴	怔	fear, apprehension, tremor.
	慄	same.
²	憐	compassion, pity; to pity, to commiserate; to love.
⁴	戀	warm affection for, attachment to, hankering after. See *lüan*⁴.
	慮	to think; thoughts; anxiety, concern; to desire; to plan; suspicion.
⁴	戀	warm affection for, attachment to, hankering after. See *lien*⁴.
⁴	慢	slowly, leisurely, easily, negligently; disrespectful, rude; proud.
ŋ²	忙	busy, hurry, hurried, pressed, fluttered; occupation.
⁴	悶	sorry, grieved, melancholy, sad.
⁴	憫	vexation, grief.
g¹	懵	obscure; undiscerning; afraid.
³	恼	shy, timid; to consider.

min³	憫	grief, sorrow, pity; to pity, to feel for.
mu⁴	慕	to respect, to esteem, to admire; devotion for; to wish for, to hanker after.
nao³	惱	vexation, shame, indignation, trouble, annoyance.
ni⁴	嬺	vicious, wicked, filthy, licentious, lewd.
nien⁴	念	to think, to study, to consider; the thoughts; to read.
nin²	您	you, sir.
no⁴	懦	imbecile, infirm of purpose, weak, timid, apprehensive, fearful.
nu⁴	怒	anger, rage, passion, to be angry with.
o⁴	惡	vicious, wicked, bad, noxious, coarse, filthy, ugly. See wu⁴.
ou⁴	慪	to provoke; respectful, reverential.
p'a⁴	怕	to fear, to apprehend, to imagine, to suppose.
pai⁴	憊	wearied, exhausted, extreme lassitude.
pei¹	悲	mournful, sad, sympathy; to pity, to commiserate, to sympathize.
pei³	悟	confident dependence on.
pei⁴	悖	perverse, disobedient, rebellious; anarchy, confusion, violence.
pên⁴	体	silly, stupid, simple, dull, unintelligent.
pi⁴	必	must; requisite, necessary, necessarily, absolutely; decision.
pieh¹	憋	vicious, bad; evil circumstances; sad; hasty temper; hurried manner.
p'ing²	憑	to lean upon, to depend on; proof, in proof of; at the pleasure of; according to. See 憑.
shên⁴	慎	careful, cautious, attentive; respectful; thoughtful; sincere; still.

shih⁴	恃	to trust to, to rely upon; depending on; to presume on. See *ssŭ⁴*.
shu⁴	恕	to shew mercy, to forgive, to excuse; indulgent, considerate, benevolent.
ssŭ¹	思	to think, to consider; to wish, to desire.
ssŭ⁴	恃	to depend on, to trust to. See *shih⁴*.
tai⁴	怠	slow, lazy, negligent, careless, inattentive, remiss; supercilious.
t'ai⁴	態	to reflect; behaviour, gait, manner, figure; an idea.
t'an³	忐	afraid, timorous; inconstant.
t'ê⁴	忒	special, particular; to exceed; to change, to alter; to err; to doubt.
t'ê⁴	忒	infirm of purpose, timidity; palpitation of the heart.
t'i³	悌	duty of younger to elder brothers.
tien⁴	惦	to be anxious about, to think kindly of.
t'ien³	忝	shy, timid, ashamed.
to⁴	惰	lazy, idle, lounging; remiss, disrespectful.
tun¹	惇	sincere, staunch, honest.
tung³	懂	to understand, clear perception of.
t'ung⁴	慟	the feelings moved to excess, extreme grief.
ts'an²	慙	to be ashamed, shame, to blush.
ts'an²	慚	same.
ts'an³	慘	grieved, pained; misery; cruel, barbarous, inhuman.
tsê⁴	惻	to commiserate, to pity, to sympathize.

tsên³	怎	what? how? why?
tsêng¹	憎	to dislike, to hate.
ts'un³	忖	to consider, to conjecture, to surmise.
tzŭ¹	恣	intrigue; levity; loose, profligate; to wish.
t'zŭ²	慈	kind, tender, compassionate; mercy, benevolence; love, to love.
wang⁴	忘	to forget; to be lost; disregarded; absence of mind.
wei²	惟	to consider; to plan, to scheme; to have; to be; is; but; only, only that; superiors.
wei⁴	慰	to soothe, to console, to comfort.
wu³	忤	undutiful, disobedient, rebellious, stubborn, obstinate.
wu³	悟	to notice, to perceive, to feel, to understand.
wu⁴	惡	to hate; abominable, detestable. See o⁴.
wu⁴	悞	to leave undone, to fail in doing, to neglect; deceitful, false; erroneous; to deceive.
yang⁴	恙	sorrow, grief, care, sickness.
yin¹	慇	mournful, sympathizing; industrious.
ying¹	應	ought, should, right, proper; to answer, to respond to. See ying⁴.
ying⁴	應	to answer, to respond to, echo; to echo. See ying¹.
yü²	愉	delicate, effeminate, luxurious; pleased; joy, delight.
yü²	愚	stupid, simple, ignorant; I.
yü⁴	愈	to get the better of, to heal; more; better; to advance.
yü⁴	慾	to desire, to wish for, to covet; lust, passion.

yüan²	忖	to measure, to estimate.
yüan⁴	愿	sincere, virtuous, moral, reverent, respectful. Used often for 願.
yüan⁴	怨	ill-will, dissatisfaction, resentment, hatred, enmity, vexed, anger.
yüeh⁴	悅	to rejoice, pleased, gratified, glad, delighted, delightful.
yu¹	憂	sorrow, sadness, grief, melancholy, downcast, thoughtful; sick.
yu¹	悠	mournful, sorry, thoughtful; distant, remote; vast; alas.
yung³	愿	to advise; brave, bold, adventurous, daring, courageous, firm, undaunted.

62
ko 戈

chan⁴	戰	to fight; a battle; to dread; to tremble; sexual intercourse.
ch'êng²	成	to make, to complete, to become, to effect.
chi³	戟	a lance, a spear, a trident; related to, relations.
ch'i⁴	戚	mournful, sorry; angry; related to, relations.
ch'iang⁴	戧	a prop; to prop (as a house, wall, &c.)
chieh⁰	截	to cut asunder or off; to be cautious, to watch.
chieh⁴	戒	to beware of, to be cautious, to watch.
ch'o³	戳	to stab, to pierce; to stamp.
'huo⁴	或	uncertain, perhaps, or, either, if.
hsi⁴	戲	theatricals; to play, to sport, to trifle, to ridicule.
hsü¹	戌	horary character; 9 to 11 o'clock P.M.

jung²	戎	a weapon; to campaign; military.
ko¹	戈	a spear, a lance.
lu⁴	戮	to kill, to execute; to hack, to mangle; foolish conduct; disgrace.
mao⁴	戊	one of the "ten stems;" earth.
shu⁴	戍	sent to the frontiers; banishment, transportation.
tai⁴	戴	to wear on the head; to bear, to sustain; to meet, to occur.
wo³	我	I, me, my, our.

63
'hu 戶

fang²	房	a house, a room, an office.
'hu⁴	戶	a door; an opening, a hole, an orifice; a family; the master.
'hu⁴	扈	the tail; to follow; a following, an escort, a guard, a train.
lei²	戾	crime, fault; perverse, impenitent; to stoop, to bend; crooked; to stop.
pien³	扁	flat; a tablet; low; small.
so³	所	a place; a thing; a cause or means; that which; the things which; relative pronoun.
shan⁴	扇	a fan; leaf of a door.

64
shou 手

ai²	挨	to receive, to suffer; side by side.
an⁴	按	to press with the hand; to examine; according to.

cha¹	扎	to thrust; to pluck up; to tie.
cha³	拃	a span.
ch'a¹	插	to stick into, to pierce, to insert.
chai¹	摘	to pluck, to pull off.
ch'ai¹	拆	to break open, to pull down, to demolish.
ch'an¹	攙	to mix up, to mingle; to support.
chang³	掌	the palm of the hand; to superintend, to control.
chang³	撐	to push; a prop; to set apart; to distribute to.
chao¹	招	to invite; to beckon; to call; a hand-bill.
chao³	找	to seek; to supply what is deficient.
chao⁴	掉	to row.
ch'ao¹	抄	to copy; to confiscate.
chê²	折	to break off; to deduct, to diminish. See shê².
chê²	摺	to fold up; a paper folded up; despatch for the Emperor.
ch'ê³	扯	to pull, to drag.
ch'ê⁴	撤	to remove, to put aside, to reject, to send away.
ch'ê⁴	掣	to drag or pull; to draw lots.
chên⁴	振	to move, to agitate; to raise; to stimulate; to save.
chêng⁴	掙	to make an effort, to try, to struggle; to earn.
ch'êng¹	撐	to push with a pole; to scull or row.

ch'ĕng²	承	to help; to receive from; to entrust to; to obey.
chi³	擠	to push, to press upon, to crowd.
chi¹	擊	to strike, to beat, to rush against.
chi⁴	技	expert in arms, skilful; talent, ability.
chia¹	挾	to carry under the arm; to conceal.
ch'ia²	掐	to nip between the finger and thumb; to pluck.
ch'iang³	搶	to rob by violence; to stand opposed to; to snatch.
chiao³	攪	to stir up, to excite; to disturb, to annoy.
ch'iao⁴	撬	to raise, to prize or use leverage, to force open.
chieh¹	揭	to raise up; to state to; to support; to be answerable.
chieh²	接	to take, to receive; to catch; to come in succession.
chieh³	捷	to overcome; prompt, quick, rapid in action.
chien³	揃	to cut, to divide asunder; sharp-pointed.
chien³	撿	to bind; to restrict; to search; to find; to compose.
chien³	揀	to choose, to select, to discriminate.
ch'ien⁴	搴	to lead, to pull, to drag, to tow.
chih¹	搘	to prop up, to support, to uphold.
chih³	指	the finger, the toe; to point with the finger; to refer to.
chih⁴	擲	to throw, to throw away. See jĕng¹.
ch'ih²	持	to grasp, to seize, to hold fast.

ch'in²	擒	to take, to seize, to take prisoner.
ch'ing²	擎	to raise with the hand, to lift high; to salute.
chiu¹	揪	to seize, to grasp; to gather; to pull up.
cho¹	拙	unskilful, unable to learn, stupid.
cho¹	捉	to grasp, to seize, to lay hold of.
ch'o¹	捔	to strike, to push, to jar; to harpoon.
ch'ou¹	抽	to pull out, to take from, to draw forth.
ch'ou¹	搐	to shake, to convulse; spasms, convulsions; to inhale; to smoke.
chü¹	拘	to seize, to lay hold of; to embrace; adhesive.
chü⁴	據	depending on, relying on; according to; in proof of.
chü⁴	拒	to oppose, to resist, to ward off, to prevent.
chüan¹	捐	to subscribe for a public purpose; to purchase rank, &c.
chüan³	撑	to roll up; to receive; to gather in; the fist.
ch'üan⁴	拳	the closed hand, the fist.
chüeh¹	抈	to snap or break off or asunder.
chüeh²	掘	to dig (as a hole, well, &c.)
chu³	拄	to prop, to support; a prop, a support.
chua¹	撾	to beat (as a drum); to avail one's self of, to take advantage of.
chua¹	抓	to tickle, to scratch, to tear; to flatter, to cajole.
ch'uai¹	搋	to draw, to pull, to drag. See yeh⁴.

ch'uai⁴	揣	to feel, to grope; to try; to measure; to estimate.
chuan⁴	撰	to arrange, to prepare; to make; to compose; composition.
chuang⁴	撞	to beat; to rush against; to seize; to swindle, to defraud.
chui¹	推	to search; to infer. See t'ui¹.
ch'ui¹	搥	to strike (as a drum, bell, &c.)
ên⁴	揾	to press the hand upon, to keep down; to obliterate.
fan¹	翻	to upset, to turn over, to toss about.
fu²	扶	to assist, to support, to hold up, to protect.
fu³	撫	to soothe, to pacify, to conciliate, to tranquillise, to manage.
fu⁴	拂	to brush, to dust; to oppose, to thwart; perverse.
'han⁴	撼	to move, to shake; to excite.
'hua¹	搲	to scratch; to wave the hand.
'huan⁴	換	to shift, to remove, to exchange.
'hui¹	揮	to point out, to direct; to wipe; to scatter; impetuous.
'huo⁴	攉	to direct, to point out; to persuade, to seduce.
hsieh²	攜	to take by the hand, to lead.
hsien¹	掀	to raise, to lift up.
hsing³	擤	to blow the nose with a handkerchief or the fingers.
i¹	揖	to fold the hands and bow; to yield.
i³	擬	to suggest; to decide. See ni³.

i⁴	抑	to oppress; perhaps, either, whether, or, if.
jang³	攘	to reject, to throw away; to seize, to steal.
jao³	擾	to put to trouble; confusion, disorder.
jêng¹	扔	to throw, to throw away.
jêng¹	擲	same. See *chih⁴*.
jou²	揉	to rub between the hands; to bend by fire.
k'ang⁴	抗	to resist, to oppose, to thwart, to disobey; to shake.
k'ao³	拷	to beat, to torture.
k'ên⁴	掯	to extort, to oppress.
ko¹	擱	to put down, to place.
kou¹	拘	to hook; to adhere to; to grasp; to restrain.
kou⁴	搆	to pull, to drag, to draw; to scheme, to plot.
k'ou¹	搉	to lift up; to store up, to put away; to turn.
k'ou⁴	扣	to strike, to hit, to knock against; to deduct; to lead a horse.
kua⁴	挂	to suspend, to hang up; to lay by; to be separated by.
kua⁴	掛	same.
kuai³	拐	a stick, a staff; to swindle; to kidnap.
k'uai³	擓	to wipe, to rub; to scratch.
k'uei³	揆	to surmise, to conjecture, to guess, to calculate; to examine; to conclude.
k'un³	捆	to take; to beat; to bind; to tie, to work on; fine work.

| shou 手 | | 78 | |

kung³	拱	Chinese salutation; to fold the hands.
k'ung⁴	控	to strike; to pull, to draw; to acc impeach; to petition against.
k'uo⁴	擴	to enlarge; to fill; to beat, to strike.
la¹	擸	to break; noise of breaking; to take hol put to rights.
la¹	拉	to pull, to draw, to drag; to break, to d
la¹	擸	to reject, to push away; to split, to des
lan²	攔	to stop, to intercept.
lan³	攬	to hoard up; to grasp at everything.
lao¹	撈	to drag out of the water; to take; to l or out.
lei²	擂	to strike; to rub, to grind, to pound mortar.
lei⁴	攂	to strike a drum; to rub, to grind; to stone; to reprimand.
lei⁴	攂	same.
liang⁴	掠	to rob, to plunder, to take by viole punish. See lüo¹.
liao¹	撩	to grasp, to manage, to wield, to fe sustain, to support.
liao⁴	撩	to seize, to plunder; to pull together.
liao⁴	撩	same.
lo¹	擄	to tuck up; to take captive, to seize, to
lo³	擺	to split, to rend; to take, to choose, to
lo³	捋	to pick, to pluck, to take hold of; to rul
lou³	摟	to draw, to pull, to drag; to embrace, to to carry off.

lüan²	攣	to tie, to bind; to attach, as by ligatures; contraction of the hands and feet.
lün¹	拵	to choose, to select; to connect, to join together. See *lun²*.
lüo¹	掠	to rob; to plunder; to take by violence; to punish. See *liang⁴*.
lun²	拵	to choose, to select; to connect together. See *lün¹*.
lung³	攏	to collect together; to put in order; to grasp, to seize.
mên¹	捫	to take hold of, to feel; to shake; to stamp; to crush.
miao²	描	to paint, to draw, to sketch, to pourtray, to describe.
min³	抿	to soothe; disorderly.
mo¹	摸	to feel, to grasp, to touch; a form, a pattern; to imitate.
mo¹	摹	same.
mo²	摩	to feel, to touch; to rub, to grind; to press, to urge; to destroy.
mo³	抹	to rub, to brush; to obliterate, to blot; to cleanse.
mu³	拇	a finger, the thumb, the great toe.
na²	拿	to lay hold of, to seize, to take, to apprehend.
na²	拏	same.
na⁴	捺	to press upon with the hand; lines from left to right.
nang³	攘	to thrust in; to fill.
nao²	撓	to scratch; to fidget; to twist, to wrench; to disturb, to vex; to mix.
nêng⁴	挵	to act, to do; to play with, to trifle, to take liberties with.
ni³	擬	to purpose, to intend, to decide; to suggest; to guess. See *i³*.

nieh¹	揑	to hold with the fingers; to rub, to knead, to work up.
nieh¹	捻	to nip with the fingers; to take or work with the fingers. See nien³.
nien¹	拈	to pluck, to pick; to handle, to take hold of with the fingers.
nien³	攆	to expel, to turn out, to drive out.
nien³	捻	to nip, to feel with the fingers. See nieh¹.
ning³	擰	to twist, to wrench, to pull, to drag; to throw into confusion.
niu³	扭	to twist, to wring, to wrench, to turn; to grasp or collar a person.
niu⁴	拗	to seize, to grasp, to drag; to break; adherence to; perverse, obstinate.
no²	挪	to shift, to remove, to transfer; to rub.
nung⁴	搏	to prop, to support; to push down.
pa¹	捌	eight; to break open; to divide; to beat.
pa¹	扒	to pull out, to eradicate; to split, to rend; to climb.
pa²	拔	to pull out of or up, to eradicate; to grasp; to excel; to raise, to promote.
pa⁴	把	to seize, to take, to hold, to grasp; a handle, Num. of fans, &c.
pai¹	擘	to break off or open.
pai¹	擗	same.
pai³	擺	to shake; to spread; to separate; to distribute; to strike; to rouse.
pai⁴	拜	to bow; to salute; to worship; to visit, to pay one's respects to.
p'ai¹	拍	to clap, to pat, to strike, to touch.
p'ai²	排	to arrange in order, to settle; to push.

pan¹	搬	to shift, to remove, to put away.
pan⁴	拌	to quarrel; to reject, to throw away, to disregard; to separate, to divide.
pan⁴	扮	to dress up, to dress one's person.
p'an¹	攀	to drag, to draw, to pull, to lead; to climb to a higher place.
p'an¹	扳	same.
pao⁴	抱	to nurse, to hold in the arms, to embrace, to enfold, to cherish; to feel.
p'ao¹	拋	to throw; to let go suddenly; to put down; to spread out.
p'ei¹	披	to carry on one; to open; to spread out; to cover over; to cast off. See p'i¹.
p'êng³	捧	to hand up; to hold up with both hands; to receive.
p'i¹	披	to open; to spread out; to cover over; to pull off; to break. See p'ei¹.
p'i¹	批	to write; to cuff; to push away; to give an official reply; a petition.
p'i³	擗	to bend, to break, to pluck off; to open; to separate from; to drive away.
piao¹	摽	to strike, to beat; to fall; to signalize.
p'ieh¹	撇	to skim; to throw away; to abandon; to strike; to wipe; to pull.
p'ieh¹	擎	same.
p'in⁴	拼	to brush or sweep away; to reject; to grasp; to stake or risk one's life.
po¹	撥	to separate, to disperse; to reject; to expel; to turn round; to spread out; to regulate.
po³	播	to winnow; to remove; to sow, to scatter, to disperse, to disseminate.
pu³	捕	to take, to seize, to apprehend; to strike; to pursue.
pu⁴	捅	to disperse, to scatter; to open out, to expand; to feel; to strike.

p'u¹	撲	to strike, to flog, to pat; to grasp; to fall; to thrust away.
sa¹	撒	to scatter, to disperse, to set loose, to throw from one, to let go.
sai²	揌	to choose, to select; to move, to agitate.
sang³	搡	to strike; to oppose, to resist.
sao³	掃	to brush, to sweep; to cast away; to suppress.
so¹	揀	to select; to pull out; to infer; to draw slowly towards one.
so¹	挱	to pat, to stroke, to rub.
so¹	抄	same.
sou¹	搜	to search, as the person, &c., to shake, to toss about.
sou³	擞	to shake, to agitate, in order to throw off.
sun³	損	to injure, to spoil; to lessen, to diminish; to lose.
shai¹	擂	to beat or roll, as a gong, &c.
shan¹	搧	to fan, to brush off, to agitate.
shan⁴	擅	to venture, to dare, to presume; to assume; to usurp, to maintain.
shê²	折	to break off, to deduct; to diminish; to fail, to lose. See *che²*.
shê³	捨	to allow to go, to part with; to reject, to forsake, to throw away.
shih²	拾	ten; to pick up; to collect, to gather together; to put in order.
shih⁴	拭	to wipe, to dust off, to rub, to cleanse.
shou³	手	the hand; to handle.
shou⁴	授	to give or deliver to.

shuaï³	摔	to throw or dash down.
shuan¹	拴	to tie up, as animals or things.
ssŭ¹	撕	to tear, to split, to cut asunder; to rouse; to point out, to direct.
ta²	搭	to add to; addition; to raise; to build; to strike; to touch; to suspend; to lean upon.
ta³	打	to strike, to beat, to lash, to fight; doing, performing; from.
t'a⁴	撻	to strike, to beat, to chastise.
t'ai²	擡	to carry on the shoulders; to lift, to raise; to move, to shake.
t'ai²	拍	same.
tan¹	擔	a pole; to bear on the shoulders; to sustain; to undertake; to be responsible for.
tan³	担	same; to strike or brush aside.
t'an¹	探	to examine, to pry, to spy, to search, to enquire, to feel, to try.
t'an¹	攤	to contribute to; to open, to spread out, to arrange; a stall; slow, remiss.
t'an²	撣	to tap, to dust; to grasp; to play on a stringed instrument.
tang³	擋	to oppose, to withstand, to impede, to obstruct; to screen; to beat.
tang³	攩	same.
t'ang²	搪	to ward off a blow; to stretch, to extend.
tao³	搗	to pound, to beat.
tao³	擣	to reel, to wind; to beat, to pound.
t'ao²	掏	to clean out a well, ditch, &c., to open out; to select.
tï²	抵	to oppose; to rush against, to butt; to substitute; to bear; to arrive, to reach to.

t'i²	提	to pick up, to raise up; to mention.
tiao⁴	掉	to hang (neuter); to move, to shake, to agitate.
t'iao¹	挑	to carry on the shoulder; to select, to take; to stir, to excite; to give trouble.
tieh²	揲	to fold up; to hang up; to arrange; to lay out; in folds; to collect.
t'ien¹	掂	to weigh in the hand.
t'ien¹	搌	to strike, to beat; to extend, to spread out; to lead, to draw.
t'ien⁴	掭	to work the Chinese pencil or brush on the ink slab.
t'ing³	挺	to stick up stiffly; to stretch out; to pluck forth; to exert.
to²	掇	to persuade; obedient; to take, to seize, to plunder, to snatch. See ts'o⁴.
t'o¹	托	to be beholden to; to receive, to take.
t'o¹	拖	to hang down; to light up; to drag, to pull, to lead, to track; to steer.
t'o¹	扡	same.
tou³	抖	to shake up or off; to rouse.
t'ou²	投	to hit; to throw; to present; to shew; to put into; to dip.
t'ui¹	推	to press, to urge, to push; to refuse, to decline; to arrange, to lay out. See chui¹.
tun¹	撴	to strike, to attack.
ts'a¹	擦	to rub, to wipe.
ts'a¹	搽	same.
ts'ai²	才	talent, ability.
ts'ai³	採	to cull, to gather, to pick, to take.

tsan³	揩	to put away; to pluck out of; to terminate; to stir.
tsan³	攢	same. See ts'uan².
ts'ao¹	操	to grasp, to lay hold of, to maintain.
tsĕ²	擇	to select, to choose.
ts'o¹	搓	to rub between the hands.
ts'o¹	撮	to unite; to snatch, to take; to urge; to take up with the fingers.
ts'o⁴	措	to raise; to arrange; to employ.
ts'o⁴	挫	to push down; to maltreat; to break to pieces.
ts'o⁴	掇	to regulate. See to².
tsuan⁴	揝	to grasp; to move, to stir.
ts'uan¹	攛	to tempt, to persuade.
ts'uan²	攢	to pile up; to collect together; to cover over; to coffin without burying. See tsan³.
ts'uan²	攢	same.
tsun³	撙	to practise; to adjust; to restrain, to manage; to collect together.
wa¹	挖	to scoop or hollow out.
wan³	挽	to bend, to force round; to pull; to lead; to draw.
wan⁴	捥	the wrist; to turn, to twist.
wo⁴	握	to close, to cover up; to put the hand on; to grasp; to take a handful. See wu³.
wu³	握	same.
ya¹	押	to guard, to escort; to suppress; to sign and seal; to pawn; to reserve.

yang²	揚	to raise high; to hold up; to spread out; to extend; to excite; to winnow; to make.
yao²	搖	to shake, to move, to wave; to imitate.
yeh¹	挨	to hold up, to assist, to support; to lean against.
yeh⁴	拽	to pull, to drag, to lead, to draw. See *chuai⁴*.
yen³	掩	to screen, to conceal; to shade, to shut; to stroke.
yi¹	揖	to fold the hands and bow; to yield. See *i¹*.
yüan²	援	to assist, to rescue, to deliver, to save; to raise up; to lead.
yung³	擁	a crowd; to crowd; to screen; to embrace; to grasp; to protect.

65
chih 支

chih¹	支	a branch; to send; to use; to pay, to branch off; to forestall.
yu¹	攲	that, what, which, who.

66
p'u 攴

ao⁴	敖	proud, haughty, uncivil.
chêng⁴	政	to regulate, to rule; ruled by government.
chiao¹	教	to teach, to instruct; a doctrine; a sect; to command.
ch'iao¹	敲	to strike, to beat, to knock, as at a door.
ching⁴	敬	sedate, respectful; to respect, to venerate.
chiu³	救	to succour, to rescue, to save, to cure.
fang⁴	放	to place, to put down; to release, to let go; to send or promote to.

fu²	敷	ample, sufficient; to diffuse, to spread.
hsiao⁴	效	like, to imitate; to respond to; according to.
kai³	改	to change, to alter, to reform.
kan³	敢	to venture, to dare; daring, bold, intrepid, rash.
ku⁴	故	a cause, because, therefore; on purpose; old; to die.
kung¹	攻	to assault, to attack; to rouse; to put in order; good; strong.
lien⁴	斂	to collect, to amass, to hoard up; to harvest; to reap.
min³	敏	quick of perception, acute; grave, serious, respectful; the great toe.
pai⁴	敗	to break, to spoil, to ruin; defeat; damaged, destroyed.
pi⁴	敝	mean, vile, bad; ragged; poor; spoiled; my; our; to desist.
pi⁴	斃	to suppress; to be killed, to die, to fall down dead.
san⁴	散	to disperse, to scatter, to let go, to dissipate, to distribute, to break up.
shou¹	收	to collect; to receive, to take; to recover; to put away; to rouse.
shu⁴	數	several, some, a few, a number; to number, to reckon, to count.
ti²	敵	an opponent, an enemy; an equal; to attack, to oppose.
tun¹	敦	sound, staunch, generous, substantial; to impel; to press upon; to rouse; large.

67
wên 文

pan²	斑	streaks, stripes; spotted; variegated.
wên²	文	ornament; literature, letters, classical; veins, streaks; ripples; civil officers.

68
tou 斗

chên¹	斟	to pour out; to deliberate and adjust.
'hu²	斛	a square corn measure (ten 斗).
hsieh²	斜	sloping, aslant, oblique, awry.
liao⁴	料	to measure; to estimate, to calculate; to suppose; materials; to manage; capacity; to consider.
tou³	斗	a measure; a peck, ten *shêng*; a star.

69
chin 斤

chan³	斬	to cut asunder, to behead.
ch'ih⁴	斥	to expel, to drive away, to reject.
chin¹	斤	the Chinese pound, a catty (1⅓ pound English); an axe.
fu³	斧	an axe or hatchet.
hsin¹	新	fresh, new, recent; to renew, to renovate, to restore.
ssŭ¹	斯	this; that; these; forthwith, immediately.
tuan⁴	斷	to cut asunder, to break; to decide, to determine, to settle; decidedly, absolutely.

70
fang 方

ch'i²	旗	a flag, banner or standard; a tribe or clan.
ching¹	旌	a banner; to signalize; to illustrate.

fang¹	方	square; then; a region, a quarter; a prescription.
hsüan²	旋	to return; to revolve; to surround; afterwards, then, next.
lü³	旅	a stranger, a guest; brothers; an assemblage; 500 men; a road, a path.
mao²	旄	a tail used as a sort of banner, a flag.
p'ang²	旁	the sides; by the side; near to.
pei⁴	旆	banners, streamers, flags.
shih¹	施	to use, to employ; to act; to arrange, to spread out; to transfer; to confer, to bestow.
tsu²	族	clan, tribe, family, kindred; species, class, sort.
yü²	於	in (the case of); on (such a day); than; through; to; at; proceeding out of; from.

71
wu 无

chi⁴	旣	finished, ended; since, having.
wu²	无	no, not, wanting.

72
jih 日

an⁴	晻	gloomy, dark; secretly; mentally.
ang²	昂	to raise, to elevate, to increase.
chan⁴	暫	a short time, temporary; the time being.
ch'ang¹	昌	abundant, affluent; increasing in strength.
ch'ang⁴	暢	to grow, to increase; joy, contentment.
chao¹	昭	bright, luminous, manifested.

ch'ên²	晨	the morning; bright, clear.
chih³	旨	the meaning or import of; imperial will; orders.
chih⁴	智	wise, wisdom, knowledge, skill, talent, ability; sharp, shrewd.
ching¹	晶	bright, clear; crystal.
ching³	景	view, prospect, appearance of; circumstances.
ch'ing²	晴	a cloudless sky, clear, fine.
chou⁴	晝	daylight, in the daytime.
ch'un¹	春	spring; wantonness, licentiousness, sensual, lustful.
'han⁴	旱	dry, drought, want of rain.
'hao²	昊	a bright summer sky, the sky, heaven.
'hun¹	昏	twilight, dusk, obscure, dull, gloomy, dim; a wife's father; marriage.
hsi¹	晰	clear, bright, distinct; to explain clearly; explicitness.
hsi²	昔	formerly, a long time ago, anciently.
hsia²	暇	leisure, unoccupied, disengaged.
hsiao³	曉	light, clear; the morning; to know, to understand; intelligent.
hsien¹	暹	Siam; the sun rising with splendour.
hsing¹	星	a star; a spark; a fortune-teller.
hsün²	旬	a decade either of days or years.
i⁴	易	alteration, change; to exchange; easy, easily. See yi⁴.
jih⁴	日	the sun; the day.

k'uang⁴	曠	clear, bright; empty, vacant, waste; distant, remote; of long duration.
kuei¹	晷	a sun-dial.
k'un¹	昆	together, at the same time; an elder brother; to take precedence.
li⁴	曆	signs of the heavens; motions of the heavenly bodies.
liang⁴	晾	to air, to dry in the sun.
mei⁴	昧	stupid, dull, obscure.
ming²	明	bright, clear; intelligent, plain; brilliant, brightness, clearness; to illustrate.
mu⁴	暮	evening, night.
nuan⁴	暖	warm, temperate, genial, soft, mild, gentle, bland.
pao⁴	暴	fierce, passionate, cruel; a storm, a tempest; scorching rays of the sun.
pu¹	晡	3 to 5 o'clock P.M.
p'u³	普	universal; great; pervading; day everywhere alike.
shai⁴	晒	to air in the sun; scorching rays of the sun.
shai⁴	曬	same.
shang³	晌	noon.
shêng¹	昇	to ascend; the sun ascending; tranquil, peaceful.
shih²	時	time; the seasons; an hour, or two hour's period; an occasion; to time rightly.
shih⁴	是	is, yes, am, are, to be; right, straight, direct; that, this, these.
shu³	暑	hot weather, sun-heat.
tan⁴	旦	morning, sunrise; clear, bright; first day of the year.

tsao²	早	the morning; early; soon; beforehand, previous.
tso²	昨	yesterday.
wan³	晚	evening; late, too late.
wang⁴	旺	brilliancy; great success; prosperous.
yi⁴	易	change, alteration; to exchange; easy, easily. See i⁴.
ying⁴	映	clear, bright, shining, dazzling.
yün¹	暈	dizzy, giddy; vapour, halo, fog and clouds.

73
yüeh 曰

ching¹	更	the night watches. See keng¹.
ch'ü¹	曲	crooked, bent, distorted; oppressed; songs.
'ho²	曷	why? why not?
'hui⁴	會	to unite, to assemble; an association or club; to be able to; to know.
kêng¹	更	to change, to alter; the night watches; more. See ching¹.
shu¹	書	a book, books; writings, letters, documents; to write characters.
t'i⁴	替	to supp'y the place of, for, instead of, on behalf of; to.
ts'ao²	曹	a meeting place; of the same place, order or class; plural.
tsêng¹	曾	past (in time); already done.
tsui⁴	最	extremely, exceedingly, very; much; important; altogether; in the highest degree.
yüeh⁴	曰	to say, to speak; to call, to denominate; to vomit; said, called, denominated.

74
yüeh 月

chao¹	朝	the morning. See ch'ao².
ch'ao²	朝	a court; a dynasty; the sovereign. See chao¹.
chên⁴	朕	I; We (of royalty, used by the Emperor alone.)
ch'i¹	期	a fixed period, a set time, a time agreed on; to expect.
fu²	服	to use; to assist; to submit, to obey; a dose of medicine; clothes.
la⁴	臘	to bind; winter month (12th.)
lang³	朗	clear, bright; lofty.
p'êng²	朋	a friend, an acquaintance.
so⁴	朔	to begin, to commence; first day of the moon.
shuo⁴	朔	same.
wang⁴	望	to look towards; to hope, to expect; towards, fronting, opposite; the full moon.
yüeh⁴	月	the moon; a month.
yu³	有	to be; to have, to possess, to attain; possession; existence; more; farther; truly.

75
mu 木

an⁴	案	an official table; a case in law; to try; to record; on record.
cha⁴	柵	a railing, a barrier.
ch'a²	查	to examine, to search, to investigate, to enquire into. Same as 察.

ch'a⁴	杈	a forked branch, a stump.
ch'ai²	柴	fuel, firewood.
chan⁴	棧	a warehouse, store-house or godown.
chang⁴	杖	a staff; to beat with the bamboo.
chên¹	榛	a kind of hazel.
chên³	枕	a pillow.
chi¹	機	a machine, a loom; to revolve; springs, motives; opportunity.
chi²	極	the utmost, the farthest point, extreme.
chi⁴	棘	a kind of thorny bush used for making fences; to fence.
ch'i¹	栖	a roost, a perch; a dwelling place; to roost or perch.
ch'i¹	柒	seven. Same as 七.
ch'i²	棊	the game of chess; a root or foundation.
ch'i²	棋	same.
ch'i⁴	棄	to break off; to throw away, to abandon, to reject.
chia⁴	枷	the wooden collar worn by Chinese criminals.
chia⁴	架	a stand, as a flower-stand, book-stand, &c.
ch'iang¹	槍	a lance, a spear.
chiao¹	椒	pepper.
chiao⁴	校	to examine, to compare; a rank.
ch'iao²	樵	a wood-cutter.

ch'iao²	橋	a bridge.
chien³	柬	to discriminate; to abridge; an abridgement; a statement.
chih¹	枝	the branch of a tree; Numerative of flowers, &c.
chih¹	梔	a fruit used for dyeing saffron colour; a flower.
chiu¹	柩	a corpse in a coffin.
cho¹	桌	a table.
cho¹	棹	same.
chü²	橘	the orange or pomelo.
ch'üan²	權	power; authority; responsibility; circumstances; weights.
chüeh²	橛	a wooden peg.
chu¹	朱	vermilion, red.
chu¹	株	the trunk of a tree; Numerative of trees.
chu⁴	柱	a post or pillar; to support, to sustain.
ch'u¹	樞	a hinge; central; indespensable, fundamental; to distress the mind.
ch'u²	櫥	a cupboard, a press, cabinet or wardrobe.
ch'u³	楚	plain, distinct, clear, sharp, defined.
ch'uan²	椽	beams, rafters. See yüan².
chuang¹	樁	a post, a pile; Numerative of affairs.
ch'un¹	椿	name of a tree, the leaves of which are eatable; a father. *Camellia japonica*.
'hang²	杭	name of a place (Hangchow.)

‘hêng²	橫	horizontal, crosswise ; perverse, obstinate.
‘ho²	核	a kernel, a walnut ; to calculate ; the facts.
‘huai²	槐	a kind of ash tree.
hsi¹	栖	a perch, a roost ; to perch ; to rest, to desist, to stop.
hsiao¹	梟	to hang the human head on the pole ; name of bird. a screech owl.
hsiao⁴	校	Imperial sedan bearers or body-guard.
hsieh⁴	械	general name for weapons.
hsing⁴	杏	the apricot or almond.
hsiu³	朽	to rot ; rotten, stinking, offensive ; forgotten.
hsüan⁴	楦	a shoemaker's last.
i²	椅	a chair.
jan³	染	to dye, to stain, to affect, to infect, to pollute to defile, to soil.
jên⁴	椹	the mulberry fruit.
jou³	柔	soft, tender, yielding, delicate, pliable, gentle.
jung²	榮	honour, rank, glory, gay, brilliant, splendid.
kai⁴	概	collectively, generally ; a strike ; to level, adjust.
kai⁴	檕	same.
k‘ai³	楷	round text ; a pattern, a mould, an example.
kan¹	杆	a stick, a post, a flag-staff ; balustrades, railing
kan¹	柑	a kind of orange.

*kan*³	桿	a post, a flag-staff; Num. of spears.
*k'an*³	欄	railings; threshold of a door.
*kang*⁴	槓	a porter's pole; pole of a sedan chair; to carry.
*kang*⁴	杠	same.
*kao*³	槁	a pole, an oar; to pole a boat; rotten.
*kên*¹	根	the root of a tree; source, origin, foundation.
*kêng*¹	梗	stem of a plant, flower, &c.
*ko*²	格	a bound or rule; to understand; able to; to reach.
*ko*²	槅	a partition, a screen; a press or case; a kernel.
*k'o*²	棵	numerative of trees.
*kou*³	枸	a fruit (a kind of medlar.)
*k'u*¹	枯	rotten wood, a dead tree; decayed, rotten, putrid.
*kuai*³	枴	a staff, a walking-stick.
*kuan*¹	棺	a coffin; to close or shut up.
*k'uang*²	框	the end of a coffin.
*kuei*⁴	櫃	a box, a press, a counter, a cabinet, a wardrobe.
*kuei*⁴	桂	cassia.
*kun*⁴	棍	a stick, a staff.
*kuo*³	果	really, truly; to surpass, to exceed; to overcome; naked, bare; fruit.
*lan*²	欄	a rail, a railing, a balustrade.

lan³	欖	the olive.
lang²	榔	the betel-nut.
lǒ⁴	樂	joy, delight, pleasure. See yo⁴.
lěng²	楞	a corner, an edge; the highest beam; a square piece of timber.
lěng⁴	棱	same.
li²	梨	the pear.
li³	李	plums; to arrange (as for a journey.)
li⁴	栗	the chesnut; firm, enduring, commanding, severe.
liang²	樑	the spine; a horizontal beam.
liang²	標	same.
lin²	林	a grove, a wood, a forest, a clump of trees; many.
lin³	檁	a cross-beam.
ling²	欞	the cross-bar of windows, &c.
liu²	榴	the pomegranate.
liu²	柳	the willow; pleasure.
lou²	樓	an upper story; a tower.
lu³	櫓	a large oar, a scull.
lu⁴	轆	a windlass for raising water; a block, a pulley.
lung³	櫳	a cage; a railing.
mei²	梅	prunes, plums, the prune species.

mei²	楣	lintel of a door; ribs of a ship; eaves of a house.
mei²	枚	a sapling, a switch; a numeral particle; one; a gag.
miao³	杪	the highest point of a tree; a twig; small, tapering.
mien²	棉	cotton.
mo²	模	a mould, a pattern. See *mu²*.
mo⁴	末	the end; the tip; the close; the last; the termination of; dust; leavings.
mou³	某	certain, as a certain man, &c.; so-and-so; I.
mu²	模	a mould, a pattern. See *mo²*.
mu⁴	木	wood; a tree.
nai⁴	柰	a fruit; kind of apple; to occur or meet with.
nan²	楠	a kind of cedar.
pa¹	杷	a handle; a rake.
pai³	柏	the cypress; large, great; to urge.
pai³	栢	same.
pan³	板	a plank, a board; a register; a kind of bastinado.
pang¹	梆	a rattle or clapper used by watchmen.
pang³	榜	to publish; a list; to propel; a splinter; a fleet.
pang⁴	棒	a drumstick, a staff, a stick, a cudgel.
pei¹	杯	a cup.
pei¹	桮	a cup; a cupboard.

mu 木

pên³	本	trunk, root, foundation, origin, source; a ment; this; I; my; our. *mu - native*
p'êng²	棚	a mat shed.
piao¹	標	to date; to insert in a book; to punctuat fathom; a signboard, a signal, a warrant
pin¹	檳	the betel-nut tree.
ping¹	梹	the betel-nut.
ping⁴	柄	a handle; having the control of; authority
p'u²	樸	unfinished utensils; untouched wood; honest.
sang¹	桑	the mulberry tree.
sên¹	森	umbrageous, luxuriant, abundant; maj commanding.
so¹	梭	a weaver's shuttle.
su²	束	to tie up, to restrain, to coerce; a bundle. See shu⁴.
sung¹	松	the fir or pine.
sha¹	杉	fir, pine.
shao²	杓	a spoon, a ladle.
shih²	柘	the pomegranate.
shih⁴	柿	a red pulpy fruit; the persimmon; the to *(original meaning)*
shu¹	梳	a comb; to comb.
shu⁴	束	to girt, to tie up, to restrain, to coerce; a bundle. See su².
shu⁴	樹	a tree; to erect; to plant.
t'a⁴	榻	a couch, a bed.

t'an²	檀	sandalwood.
tang⁴	橕	a frame; cross-beams.
t'ang²	棠	name of a kind of pear.
t'ao²	桃	the peach.
t'êng⁴	櫈	a stool, a form, a bench.
t'i¹	梯	a ladder, steps; means to an end.
tiao²	條	a branch, a twig; items; Num. of dogs, &c.
t'ing¹	梃	a bough; a staff, a stick.
to²	朵	a bud, a flower, petals; pendant; the lobe of the ear; Num. of flowers, &c.
t'o²	柁	beams (large.)
tu⁴	杜	to stop or fill up; to shoot.
tung¹	東	the east; the place of honour; spring; a master.
tung⁴	棟	pillars, posts, upright columns.
t'ung²	桐	name of a tree (dryandra.)
t'ung³	桶	a tub, a cask, a barrel, a bucket.
tsai¹	栽	to plant, to transplant.
ts'ai²	材	materials, elements.
tsao³	棗	a kind of date.
ts'ao²	槽	a trough, a manger; a wine shop.
tso⁴	柞	name of a hard-wood.

ts'un¹	村	a village, a hamlet.
tsung¹	棕	the coir palm; coir.
tsung¹	椶	same.
tzŭ²	梓	the cedar.
wang³	枉	crooked, distorted, perverted; bent d oppressed; injustice.
wei²	桅	a mast.
wei⁴	未	not, not yet, not now; 1 to 3 o'clock P.M. 6th moon.
wu¹	杇	a trowel.
wu²	樢	ebony.
wu²	梧	name of a tree (dryandra.)
wu⁴	杌	stunted; stump of a tree; a stool.
yang²	楊	a kind of poplar.
yang⁴	樣	kind, fashion, manner, way, sort; a ru pattern.
yeh⁴	業	land, property, estates; an affair; occupa meritorious service.
ying¹	樱	the cherry.
yo⁴	樂	music; any musical instrument. See lo⁴.
yü²	榆	a kind of elm.
yüan²	橼	a kind of lemon; a rafter. See ch'uan².
yu⁴	柚	the pomelo.

76
ch'ien 欠

ch'i¹	欺	to deceive, to impose on; to insult.
ch'ien⁴	欠	deficient, wanting; to owe.
ch'in¹	欽	thoughtful; respect; grand; imperial.
ch'ua¹	歘	sudden, abrupt, startled; to sniff.
'huan¹	歡	satisfaction, joy, pleasure, delight.
hsieh¹	歇	to desist, to stop, to rest, to leave off.
hsin¹	欣	joy, pleasure, delight. laughing for joy.
ko¹	歌	to sing.
k'uan³	款	real, sincere; affectionate; to extend to; to detain; empty; a sort, a class; leisurely.
t'an⁴	歎	to sigh, to moan; a sigh, a long breath.
tz̆ŭ⁴	次	second to, next in order, inferior; a time, a turn, a place; an inn.
yü⁴	欲	to wish, to hope, to desire, to covet, to long for; to be about to; just as or at.

77
chih 止

chêng¹	正	correct, straight, regular; the first, the principal.
chêng³	整	whole, complete, entire; to repair, to adorn.
chih³	止	to stop, to desist, to be still, to rest.

kuei¹	歸	to belong to; to revert, or return to; to add to; to attach to; addition.
li⁴	歷	to pass by, over, to or through; progressive.
pu⁴	步	a pace; to pace, to walk, to go; to go on foot; the ways of.
sui⁴	歲	the year; the harvest; the planet Jupiter.
tz'ŭ³	此	this; these; here; now.
wai¹	歪	crooked, distorted, twisted, irregular.
wu³	武	military, martial, warlike; strong; dignified.

78

tai 歹

hsün⁴	殉	to be killed or die in the discharge of one's duty; resolution.
lien⁴	殮	to dress the dead, to enshroud.
pin⁴	殯	a funeral; to perform funeral rites, to bury.
shu¹	殊	very; to exceed; to distinguish; to wound, to kill, to exterminate.
ssŭ¹	死	to die.
tai³	歹	bad, vicious, perverse, rebellious.
tai⁴	殆	to begin; to approach, nearly, about to, on the limits of; dangerous.
ts'an²	殘	to injure, to spoil, to destroy; to rob; to mangle; wicked; cruel; deficient; leavings.
yang¹	殃	fault; punishment; calamity, judgment, ruin; to fight.
yün³	殞	to fade, to fall, to perish, to die.

79
shu 殳

'hui³	毀	to break, to ruin, to destroy; to slander.
k'o¹	殼	shell, skin, husk, &c.
kou⁴	彀	enough.
ou¹	毆	to beat, to strike; to fight with the fist; a club, a bludgeon.
sha¹	殺	to kill, to murder; to die; to seize; to overcome; to exterminate.
shu¹	殳	a weapon, a spear; to sink.
tien⁴	殿	a hall, a palace; fixed, settled; the rear of an army.
tuan⁴	段	a piece, a section, a paragraph.
yin¹	殷	wealthy, affluent; flourishing, abundant; respectable; right, correct.

80
mu 毋

mei³	每	each, every; always, constantly.
mu³	毋	mother; the female.
tu²	毒	poison; poisonous, noxious, injurious, painful; to hate.
wu²	毋	do not; a denial.

81
pi 比

pi³	比	to compare, to correspond, to equal; according with; to make, to provide, to prepare.

82
mao 毛

chan¹	毡	felt.
chan¹	氈	same.
ch'iu²	毬	a ball (such as children play with, &c.)
'hao²	毫	a small hair; fine, small, trifling, the least; a weight; a pencil.
jung²	羢	felt, cloth.
jung³	氄	down, fur; to fledge.
lu⁴	氇	a sort of hair or woollen cloth (Thibetan.)
mao²	毛	hair, feathers, down, nap; hair on the eyebrows or body; grass.
t'an²	毯	a rug, a carpet.

83
ch'i 气

ch'i⁴	氣	air, breath, vapour; temper, anger. *spirit, as ft. ghost.*
fên¹	氛	fume, vapour; noxious, pernicious, pestilential.

84
shih 氏

min²	民	the people; natives, subjects of a country (not official.)
shih⁴	氏	family name; sect, kindred, clan.

85
shui 水

ao⁴	澳	a high bank or shore; a bay.
cha¹	渣	grounds, dregs.
chan⁴	沾	to moisten, to tinge, to be affected by.
chan⁴	湛	dew; fresh as dew.
chang⁴	漲	the rising of water, to overflow.
ch'ao²	潮	the tide; damp, moist.
ch'ên²	沉	to sink; to cause to sink; weighty.
chi²	汲	to draw water out of a well; to draw forth.
chi²	激	water rushing past rocks; gratitude.
chi⁴	濟	to assist, to be beneficial to, to cause success to.
ch'i¹	沏	to pour boiling water on tea (to *make* tea.)
ch'i¹	漆	varnish, lacquer.
ch'i⁴	泣	to shed tears, to weep silently.
chiang¹	江	a river.
chiang¹	漿	syrup; any thick fluid; pus, matter; starch; to starch.
chiang³	港	a drain, a passage for water, an arm of the sea.
chiao¹	澆	to sprinkle, as in watering flowers, &c.
chieh²	潔	pure, chaste, clear, clean.

chien⁴	濺	to splash, to spatter.
chien⁴	澗	a mountain stream.
chien⁴	漸	gradually, by slow degrees, by little and little.
ch'ien²	潛	to ford, to enter deeply, to cross; to abscond; to secrete; secretly.
ch'ien³	淺	shallow, superficial, slightly.
chih¹	汁	juice, gravy, sap; rich, luscious, juicy.
chih³	治	to heal, to cure; to put in order, to direct, to govern, to punish.
chih⁴	滯	congealed, congelation, concretion; to impede.
ch'ih²	池	a pond, pool, tank or moat.
chin¹	浸	to soak, to saturate, to steep, to drench.
chin¹	津	a ford; a creek, a rivulet; to imbue, to moisten.
ching¹	津	same.
ching⁴	淨	to wash clean; clean, pure.
ch'ing¹	清	pure, limpid, clear, transparent.
ch'iu²	求	to supplicate, to beg, to entreat, to invite; to seek.
cho¹	涿	flowing down in drops, trickling.
cho²	濁	thick, foul; muddy water; obscure.
cho²	濯	to wash, to cleanse, to purify.
chou¹	洲	an island; a continent.
ch'ü²	渠	a drain, a gutter.

chüan¹	涓	a brook, a stream, a rill.
ch'üan²	泉	a spring, the source of a stream.
chüeh²	決	to flow; to settle, to decide; decided, determined.
chu⁴	注	water flowing; to record; to illustrate, to comment upon.
chun³	準	to approve, to allow, to grant; to adjust, to equalize, to fix; to weigh. See 准.
ch'ung¹	沖	to boil or burst over, as water; to wash away; to fly up; to dart.
fa²	法	method, fashion; law, rule; punishment.
fan⁴	泛	to float, to flow; to spill; to open (as flowers); common.
fou²	浮	to float, to swim; light, buoyant.
fu⁴	沸	to boil or bubble up.
'hai⁴	海	the sea.
'han²	涵	to soak; to bear; to treat leniently, to look over.
'han⁴	汗	perspiration, sweat.
'han⁴	漢	the milky way; name of a dynasty; a man; a Chinaman.
'hao⁴	浩	a broad expanse of water; great, broad, extensive.
'ho²	河	a river.
'ho⁴	涸	water dried up; exhausted.
'hu²	湖	a lake.
'hua²	滑	smooth, slippery; sharp; a drug; soap-stone.
'hun⁴	渾	muddy, polluted; mingled; the whole of, one mass.

ʿhun⁴	混	water mingled in confusion; muddy, dull.
ʿhung²	洪	a torrent, a flood; great, vast, extensive.
ʿhung⁴	汞	quicksilver, mercury, cinnabar.
ʿhuo²	活	alive, living; moving, moveable; cheerful, lively.
hsi¹	溪	a mountain stream.
hsi³	洗	to wash, to cleanse.
hsiang¹	湘	name of a district and lake.
hsiao¹	消	to thaw, to melt, to digest, to dissipate, to disperse.
hsieh⁴	瀉	purging, dysentery; to drain.
hsieh⁴	泄	to ooze, to drip out, to leak; bowel complaint; rest, sloth, idle indulgence.
hsieh⁴	洩	to leak, to ooze out; to lessen; to be appeased.
hsien²	涎	slaver, drivel; to long, to covet.
hsün⁴	汛	a military station; to guard, to protect; speed, velocity.
ju³	汝	you, yours.
jun⁴	潤	moist; to moisten; to instil into; to benefit, to enrich.
kʿo³	渴	thirsty; anxious to attain, to long for.
kou¹	溝	a gutter, a drain, a sewer, a ditch, a moat.
ku¹	沽	to buy; to sell; to lessen, to retrench, to abridge; coarse, bad.
kuan⁴	灌	to drink; to flow; to assemble, to collect together.
kʿuang⁴	況	more, further, moreover, still, besides. See 况.

kun³	滾	water bubbling or boiling; to roll, to flow.
lan²	瀾	streams flowing and blending together; thick water.
lan⁴	濫	a drain; to overflow; floating, superficial; to exceed, to encroach; loose, unsettled.
lang⁴	浪	waves; unsettled; profligate, dissipated.
lao⁴	潦	to sink in water; running water; an inundation.
lei⁴	淚	tears, weeping.
li⁴	瀝	dripping of water; to drop; to pour out.
liang²	涼	cool, pleasant; sparing; uncomfortable.
lin⁴	淋	water dripping; to drip; to wet, to soak; a pool, a pond.
liu¹	溜	to flow gently; to issue forth.
liu²	流	to flow, to glide, to descend; the course of; the progress of; to cast off; to select.
lou⁴	漏	to leak, to drip, to ooze, to let out, to disclose; an aperture; to bore; to instil; to confer.
lu³	滷	salt land; bitter; salt.
man³	滿	full; completed; enough, sufficient; all, the whole.
man⁴	漫	filled with water; flood; set loose; source of a river; colour of the clouds; a vast extent.
mei²	沒	not, there is not; to die, to perish. See mo⁴ and mu².
mêng¹	濛	mist, thick, foggy, small drizzling rain, Scotch mist.
miao³	渺	small; white; glittering; vast; indistinct.
mieh⁴	滅	to extinguish; to exterminate, to annihilate, to destroy, to cut off.
mo⁴	沫	scum, spittle, saliva.

mo⁴	沒	not, there is not; to covet; to sink; to end, to die. See *mei²* and *mu²*.
mo⁴	漠	floating sands; a sandy desert.
mu²	沒	not, there is not; to end, to die. See *mei²* and *mo⁴*.
mu⁴	沐	to wash; to enrich; to receive favours; to regulate.
nêng²	濃	mud, muddy, thick. See *nung²*.
ni²	泥	mud, muddy, thick, clammy; adhesive; stagnant; rotten; bigoted; soft.
ni⁴	溺	weak, foolish; to draw; to be sunk into; to fall in. See *niao⁴*.
niao⁴	溺	urine; to pass urine. See *ni⁴*.
nung²	濃	thick (of fluid); rich, strong. See *nêng²*.
ou⁴	漚	to steep, to soak, to saturate, to soften by steeping.
p'ai⁴	派	to send, to appoint, to distribute; to branch off.
p'an¹	潘	dregs; spots on the face.
p'ao⁴	泡	bubbles, blisters, pustules; to pour.
p'ei⁴	沛	abundant showers, rainy; increasing; large, great.
p'iao⁴	漂	tossing about, agitated, as by the wind; to float.
pin¹	濱	a shore, bank, or beach; margin of a sea, or river.
po¹	波	waves; a ruffled surface.
p'o¹	潑	to sprinkle, to scatter, to shower; water dripping out.
p'u³	浦	a creek, an inlet, a stream; a bend.
p'u³	溥	great, large; to disperse; pervading everywhere, all over the world.

sa³	洒	to sprinkle water; to wash, to cleanse; to scatter, to disperse; to fall down.
sa³	灑	same.
sê⁴	濇	rough, opposite of smooth.
sê⁴	澁	rough to the taste; rough, rugged, rippled.
so⁴	溯	to look back; a river, a stream; to think; flowing.
sha¹	沙	sand, pebbles, small stones.
shao⁴	潲	to sprinkle, to dash water; water dashing against.
shê⁴	涉	to ford, to wade across; passing through; to involve; to implicate; concerned in.
shên¹	深	deep, profound; very, extremely.
shih¹	湿	wet, damp, moist.
shih¹	濕	same.
shu²	淑	limpid, pure, uncorrupted, virtuous; accomplished.
shua⁴	涮	sound of falling rain; to rinse.
shui³	水	water.
t'ai⁴	汰	slippery; to wash, to cleanse; rushing of water; excess; to boast.
t'ai⁴	泰	great, large, excessive, extravagant, liberal, easy.
tan⁴	淡	weak, thin, watery, insipid, tasteless; pale, light; volatile.
tan⁴	澹	still, tranquil; appearance of water.
t'an¹	灘	a rapid, rushing of water; a beach.
t'an²	潭	name of a river; deep.

t'ang¹	湯	broth, soup, gravy, sauce, hot water.
t'ang³	盪	to flow; waves.
t'ao¹	滔	to flow; water gradually rising.
t'ao²	淘	to wash rice; to scour; to stir, to excite.
têng⁴	澄	clear, limpid; still, pure water.
ti¹	滴	to drop, to drip; a drop.
ti⁴	涕	tears; to shed tears; mucus.
t'ien¹	添	to lay on, to increase, to add to, additional.
tu⁴	渡	to cross over; to pass through; to ferry over.
tun⁴	沌	confused, chaotic; a torrent.
tung⁴	洞	a cave; deep, profound; a bridal chamber.
tsao³	澡	to wash, to bathe.
ts'ao²	漕	a water-wheel; to convey by water; tribute boats.
tsê²	澤	kindness; to nourish; softened; enriched; a marsh; glossy.
ts'ê⁴	測	to fathom, to measure.
ts'ou⁴	湊	to assemble, to collect together; to add to; to make up.
tzŭ¹	滋	a pleasant flavour; thick; rich; to enrich; to increase; to overflow.
tzŭ³	滓	grounds, dregs, sediment.
wa⁴	窪	low ground, swamp.
wan¹	灣	a bay, a curving; to anchor.

wang¹	汪	wide and deep; vast; a lake or pond; an ocean.
wĕn¹	溫	warm, genial, mild, benign, kind, cordial; to warm.
wu¹	汙	foul, filthy, filth, impure; to stain, to defile; degraded, low.
wu¹	污	same.
ya²	涯	the horizon; the edge; a bank, a shore.
yang²	洋	the ocean; vast, extensive; foreign.
yao²	淆	muddy water; mixed up, confused.
yen¹	淹	to drown; to soak, to saturate; to spoil.
yen²	沿	a bank, a shore, an edge; to flow; to make a tour.
yen³	演	to exercise, to practise, to make trial of, to perform.
yin²	淫	desire, lust, excess; to debauch; absence; error.
yü¹	淤	mud, muddy water; matter, pus.
yü²	漁	to fish; a fisherman.
yü⁴	浴	to bathe; to fly or skim like a swallow.
yüan¹	淵	an abyss, an eddy, a whirlpool; deep, common.
yüan²	源	a spring, a fountain. Same as 原.
yu²	油	oil, oily, greasy; grease, lard, fat.
yu²	游	to roam, to wander; to stroll; to flow, to float, to swim.
yung³	湧	to bubble up, to rise or spring up.
yung³	永	eternal, everlasting, for ever, perpetual, always.

86
‘huo 火

ao²	熬	to decoct, to boil, to distil.
cha²	煠	to fry in oil.
cha²	炸	same.
chao²	燒	to kindle; to apply fire to.
chao⁴	照	to illumine, to reflect; light; according to; like, the same as.
ch'ao³	炒	to fry or roast in a pan.
chiao¹	焦	scorched, seared; vexation, anxiety, distress.
chien¹	煎	to fry, to decoct; vexation, annoyance.
chih⁴	炙	to broil, to warm, to heat.
chin⁴	燼	the remains; the snuff of a candle; ashes.
chu²	燭	a candle; the light of a candle; to illumine.
chu³	煮	to boil, to decoct; boiled, decocted.
chu³	煑	same.
chu⁴	炷	a lampwick; Numerative of incense sticks.
ch'ui¹	炊	to boil, to cook, to steam.
fan²	煩	to trouble, troubled; annoying, vexing; grieved, sorry.
fên²	焚	to set on fire, to burn.
‘hu²	煳	to scorch, to burn.

‘huan⁴	煥	blaze, flame, light, bright.
‘huang²	煌	blaze, flame, bright, dazzling, splendid.
‘huang³	熀	to shine, to dazzle; shining, dazzling; to flash; a flash.
‘hui¹	灰	ashes; to despair; lavender or slate color.
‘hui³	燬	to burn, to set fire to.
‘hung¹	烘	to dry by a fire.
‘huo³	火	fire, fiery, heat, fever; to burn.
hsi¹	熹	hot, burning, heat; to roast, to boil.
hsi¹	熙	flourishing, prosperous; harmonizing; bright.
hsi²	熄	to extinguish.
hsiung²	熊	the bear.
hsün¹	熏	vapour, fumes, steam, evaporation.
jan²	然	yes, really, truly, naturally; done; is, am.
jan²	燃	to light, to burn, to kindle.
jê⁴	熱	warm, hot, ardent, affectionate.
k'ang⁴	炕	a stove bed; to dry by a fire.
k'ao³	烤	to warm, to roast, to toast.
lan⁴	爛	clear, bright; boiled to rags; to break, to tear; ragged, tattered.
lao⁴	烙	to burn; a red hot iron point; red hot, burning.
liao³	燎	beacon lights; a hanging lamp.

lieh⁴	烈	ardent, impetuous, enthusiastic, daring, fierce, cruel; anxious; excellent; splendid.
lien⁴	煉	to melt; to refine metals by fire.
lien⁴	鍊	same.
lu²	爐	a stove, a fire-place, a furnace, a vase for incense.
lung²	爖	fire; to light; to warm.
mei²	煤	coal.
miao⁴	焰	sparks, flame.
nuan³	煖	warm, warmth of fire.
pao⁴	爆	the sound of fireworks; to fizz; fireworks; fire bursting.
p'ao⁴	炮	to roast, to burn, to bake; a cannon; a rocket.
pei⁴	焙	to dry with fire; to hatch eggs with fire.
p'êng¹	烹	to fry, to boil.
ping³	炳	the light of fire; luminous, perspicuous, clear.
sha¹	煞	to seize; to kill, to murder. Same as 殺.
shan¹	煽	to excite; to delude; to make a flame; to act as an incendiary.
shao¹	燒	to burn, to roast, to boil.
shou²	熟	ripe, cooked, mature; well versed in, skilled; intimate, acquainted with.
shu²	熟	same.
t'an⁴	炭	charcoal, wood coals.
t'ang⁴	燙	to scald; a bath.

têng¹	燈	a light, a lamp, a lantern.
tien¹	点	a point, a particle, a dot, a spot; to punctuate; to blot, to soil; to light a candle; to nod. See 點.
tun⁴	燉	to stew.
tsai¹	灾	dangerous; calamity, misfortune; injurious, calamitous.
tsai¹	災	same.
ts'an⁴	燦	bright, clear, luminous.
tsao⁴	燥	dry, dried with fire, scorched, parched.
tsao⁴	灶	a furnace, a fire-place.
ts'uan⁴	爨	a furnace; to light a fire to cook by, to cook.
wu¹	烏	black; a crow.
wu²	無	no, not, not to be, not to have, destitute of.
yen¹	煙	tobacco; opium; smoke.
yen¹	烟	same.
yen¹	焉	how? what? don't; rest, repose.
yen²	炎	to blaze, flame, hot, burning, glorious, bright.
yen⁴	焰	glare, flame, light, bright.
yen⁴	燕	rest, repose; the swallow.
ying²	營	a barrack, an entrenchment, a cantonment; to do; to make.
yü⁴	熨	a smoothing iron; to smooth.
yün⁴	熨	same.

87

chao 爪

chao³	爪	nails of the toes or fingers, claws, talons.
chêng¹	爭	to wrangle, to quarrel, to contest, to litigate, to emulate.
chüeh²	爵	a cup; nobility, rank, high office.
p'a²	爬	to scrape, to scratch, to scrawl; to creep.
wei²	爲	to do, to be, to act as; to make; for, because of, an account of; in order that; for the sake of; the reason.

88

fu 父

fu⁴	父	a father; a title of respect.
pa⁴	爸	a father; an aged person.
tieh¹	爹	a father.
yeh¹	爺	father; a term of respect.

89

yao 爻

êrh³	爾	you, your; a response, an answer.
shuang¹	爽	lively, cheerful, hearty, comfortable; valuable; to please, to gratify; to miss; to fail.
yao²	爻	to imitate; fortune-telling books.

90
ch'iang 爿

ch'iang² 牆 a wall.

ch'uang² 牀 a bed or couch. See 床.

91
p'ien 片

chien¹ 牋 note paper. See 箋.

ch'uang¹ 牕 a window. See 窗.

p'ai² 牌 a warrant, a permit, a clearance; a card; an arch; a raft; a shield.

pan³ 版 a plank, a board; a register; a kind of bastinado.

p'ien⁴ 片 a piece, a slice, a slip, a bit, a fragment, a splinter; a petal, a leaf; to break; the half.

tieh² 牒 an official document; a genealogical register.

tu³ 牘 tablets for writing on; documents.

92
ya 牙

ya² 牙 the teeth.

93
niu 牛

ch'ien¹ 牽 to pull, to drag, to lead.

hsi¹ 犀 the rhinoceros.

lao²	牢	a prison; a pen or fold; lasting, strong.
li²	犂	a plough; to plough, to cultivate.
mu³	牡	the male of animals; a bolt.
mu⁴	牧	a shepherd, a herd, a pastor; to oversee; to feed.
niu²	牛	the ox.
p'in⁴	牝	female, female of animals, &c.; the vagina.
shêng¹	牲	cattle, beasts.
t'ê⁴	特	special, particular, especially, on purpose; alone; only; a stallion; a bullock.
wu⁴	物	things, any thing or creature; business; a class or sort.

94
ch'üan 犬

ch'ang¹	猖	fierce, wild, frightened.
chiao³	狡	artful, crafty, cunning, perverse, disorderly.
ch'ou⁴	臭	scent, perfume, smell, stink, stinking.
ch'üan³	犬	the dog.
chu¹	猪	the pig.
chuang³	狀	exterior appearance; fashion, form; to accuse; an accusation; a petition.
fan⁴	犯	to rush against; to offend; to violate the laws; an offender.
'hên³	狠	very, extremely. See 很.
'hou²	猴	the monkey.

'hu²	猢	a kind of monkey.
'hu²	狐	the fox; suspicious.
'hua²	猾	artful, crafty, lying, deceitful, disorderly.
'huan²	獾	the badger, the fat of which is used for burns, scalds, &c.
'huo⁴	獲	to capture, to apprehend; to obtain; to gather in, to harvest.
hsia²	狹	compressed, narrow, circumscribed.
hsien⁴	獻	to offer to, to present to, to hand to; offerings.
hsing¹	猩	a kind of monkey, the blood of which is used for dyeing.
hsün²	狥	to connive at, connivance.
kou³	狗	the dog.
k'uang²	狂	mad, madness, insanity; ambitious, enthusiastic.
lang²	狼	the wolf; name of a plant; to swindle.
li²	狸	the fox; the wild cat.
lieh⁴	獵	to hunt, to pursue; to have passed through; a porpoise.
mêng³	猛	fierce, cruel, savage; courageous; vehement; strong; injurious.
pei⁴	狽	a kind of wolf; embarrassment.
pi⁴	獘	fault, crime; to extort, to squeeze.
shih¹	獅	the lion.
shou⁴	獸	wild beasts of any kind; a quadruped.
t'a³	獺	the otter.

tai¹	獃	silly, idiotic, foolish. See 呆.
ti²	狄	Tartar tribes; the northern region; Mongolians.
tu²	獨	singly, alone, one's self. *also half-ape*
ts'ai³	猜	to guess, to conjecture; to dislike; to suspect.
yü⁴	獄	prison; hell; criminal cases.
yüan²	猿	the monkey or ape.
yu²	猶	irresolute, undecided, doubtful; to plan; a path; still; even; as if.
yu²	猷	same.

95
hsüan 玄

hsüan²	玄	black, sombre; gloomy.
shuai⁴	率	naturally careless; light and active; sudden action, prompt; generally.
tz'ŭ¹	兹	now; on account of, because of; the; then; but; still; initial particle.

96
yü 玉

chên¹	珍	precious, valuable, important.
ch'in²	琴	a dulcimer, a lute, a harp.
chiu³	玖	a kind of jade; nine.
ch'iu²	球	a globe, an orb, a sphere.

ch'iung²	瓊	a beautiful kind of jade.
cho²	琢	to work precious stones; to cut, to carve. See ts'o².
chu¹	珠	a pearl, a bead.
'hu²	瑚	coral.
'hu³	琥	amber.
'huan²	環	a ring, a circle; an arch; to encircle, to surround; to link.
hsi³	璽	Imperial or national seal.
hsia²	瑕	fractured, split, cracked; a flaw; error, fault, crime.
hsien⁴	現	now, the present time; visible, apparent.
jui⁴	瑞	an auspicious omen; good fortune, blessings, prosperity.
kuei⁴	瑰	a pearl; rare; precious; extraordinary.
li²	璃	glass; gloss, glare.
li³	理	reason, right, principle; to manage, to regulate, to govern, to control.
liu²	琉	a pearl, a bead; vitreous, glazed; shining, bright.
ma³	瑪	the carnelian.
mei²	玫	a red stone; mignonette.
nao³	瑙	the carnelian.
p'a¹	琶	a stringed instrument.
pan²	班	a troop, a rank, a row, a class, a gradation, a set; a turn.
pei⁴	珮	a girdle or sash with stone attached to it.

pi^4	璧	an auspicious stone.
$p'i^2$	琵	a sort of guitar.
po^1	玻	glass.
$p'o^4$	珀	amber.
$sê^4$	瑟	a kind of harp; numerous, many; stern.
so^3	瑣	small, minute; trifles, small things; broken stones.
$shan^1$	珊	coral.
$tien^4$	玷	a flaw, a blot, a blemish; to disgrace.
$ts'o^2$	琢	to work jewels; to cut, to carve; to choose, to select. See cho^2.
wan^2	玩	a precious stone; to play, to trifle; to take delight in; to seduce; childish. See 頑.
$wang^2$	王	a prince, a king.
$ying^1$	瑛	glitter of gems.
$ying^2$	瑩	glitter of gems; bright, shining; clearness of perception.
$yü^2$	玉	jade, jewels; precious, valuable; beautiful.

97

kua 瓜

$jang^2$	瓤	the edible part of a melon; the inside, the core.
kua^1	瓜	cucumbers, melons, gourds, &c.
pan^4	瓣	the section of a melon, orange, &c.; petals.
$piao^4$	瓢	a calabash.

98
wa 瓦

chuan¹	甎	bricks, tiles or flags.
p'ing²	瓶	a bottle, a vase.
tsêng⁴	甑	a boiler.
wa¹	瓦	tiles, bricks or flags.
wêng⁴	甕	a wine jar.

99
kan 甘

kan¹	甘	sweet; pleasant, agreeable; voluntary.
shên²	甚	extremely, very; social delights; excess of pleasure.
t'ien²	甜	sweet; excellent.
t'ien²	甛	same.

100
shêng 生

ch'an³	產	to produce, to bear; an estate; property.
su¹	甦	to revive, to resuscitate, resuscitation.
shêng¹	生	to bear, to produce, to be born; human life; unripe, new, raw; present or future.
shêng¹	甥	a sister's son; a daughter's children or husband; a wet nurse.

101
yung 用

fu³	甫	great; many; a head; an appellation.
yung³	甬	passing through; a lane.
yung⁴	用	to use, to employ, to partake of; the necessary expense; by; with.

102
t'ien 田

chi¹	畸	odds and ends; bits of waste land.
ch'i²	畦	small beds or plots of ground.
chia³	甲	to begin; the first; armour, scales; finger nails.
chiang¹	疆	a boundary, frontier or limit.
chieh⁴	界	a boundary, a frontier, a ridge, a limit; to limit.
ch'u⁴	畜	any domesticated animals. See hsü¹.
fan¹	番	a time, a turn, a repetition of; wild, barbarous.
hsü¹	畜	to feed, to nourish; to collect together. See ch'u⁴.
i⁴	異	different; from; separated; strange, odd, unusual, wonderful.
liao⁴	畧	a boundary, a partition; to share; a plan; to visit; a little.
liao⁴	略	same.
liu²	留	to stop; to keep, to detain, to delay; slowly, leisurely; a long time.
mu³	畝	the Chinese acre.

nan²	男	male; 5th title of nobility; a baron.
pi⁴	畢	the end, close, termination, at last; finished, completed.
shên¹	申	3 to 5 o'clock P.M.; to explain, to clear up; to reiterate.
tang¹	當	to suit, to be fit; suitable, right, proper, ought; to represent; to bear; to pawn, to pledge. *in, at*.
tieh²	疊	in many folds or layers; to pile up; to reiterate.
t'ien²	田	a field; land, ground.
wei⁴	畏	to fear, to dread, to venerate; awe, reverence; assiduity, diligence.
yu²	由	from, proceeding from; through; to let; to depend upon.

103
p'i 疋

i²	疑	to doubt, to suspect; to guess, to suppose; doubt, suspicion.
p'i³	疋	a piece, a bale; Num. of pieces of cloth, &c.
su²	疎	distant, far.
su²	疏	same.

104
ni 疒

chên³	疹	a skin disease, a kind of rash, measles.
chêng⁴	症	illness, sickness.
chi²	疾	sudden illness; any sickness; quick; a trouble.
chi²	瘵	consumption; weary; sick.

chieh¹	癤	a sore, an ulcer, a tumour.
chieh⁴	疥	the itch.
chih⁴	痔	hæmorrhoids, piles.
chih⁴	痣	a spot; a mole.
ch'ih²	痴	foolish, simple, idiotic.
ch'ih²	癡	same.
ch'ou¹	瘳	convalescent, well, cured.
chü¹	疽	an old sore; deeply rooted; faults, &c., of long standing.
ch'üan²	痊	to cure, cured, convalescent, recovered.
ch'üeh²	瘸	lameness.
ch'uang³	瘡	any sore or ulcer.
fei⁴	痱	prickly heat, pimples.
fei⁴	癈	chronic, incurable.
fêng¹	瘋	insane, insanity; paralysis.
'hên²	痕	a scar, a mark, a trace.
'hou²	瘊	a spot, a pimple, a wort.
'huan⁴	瘓	palsy, paralysis (on the right side.)
'huang²	癀	the yellow jaundice.
'huo⁴	癨	a kind of colic or cholera.
üan³	癬	a skin disease; ringworm.

i⁴	疫	an epidemic, plague, pestilence, distemper. See yi⁴.
kan¹	疳	a sort of spreading sore, venereal sores.
ko¹	疙	pimples, boils; silly, idiotic.
la¹	瘌	poison; pain; a hurt; an itching sore; a scar.
lai⁴	癩	a virulent disorder or sore; itch.
lao²	癆	emaciated, consumptive, declining.
li⁴	痢	purging, dysentery, flux.
liao⁴	療	to cure; the practice of medicine.
liu²	瘤	a swelling, a tumour, a wen.
lo³	瘰	a gathering, a fester; glands of the ears swelling.
lou⁴	瘺	an ulcer, a swelling, an old sore.
ma³	痲	the small-pox.
pa¹	疤	a scar, a cicatrice.
pan²	瘢	a scar, marks, marks of the small-pox.
pêng¹	痭	dropsy, swelling of the stomach.
p'i²	疲	fatigued, wearied, exhausted; weakness, lassitude, inability.
p'i³	痞	a craving appetite; spitting of phlegm; indigestion.
p'i³	痦	pain; disease; a gathering; a stoppage; weak, debilitated.
pieh¹	癟	to suppress, to keep down; a swelling that has burst.
pieh³	癟	decay; distorted; toothless.

ping⁴	病	illness, disease, sickness; defect, fault.
shan³	疝	wind in the stomach; a belly rupture.
shou⁴	瘦	thin, lean, emaciated.
ta²	瘩	a knot; a sore, a scab.
tai⁴	帶	the whites.
t'an¹	癱	paralysis, palsy, contraction of the muscles.
t'an²	痰	phlegm.
t'êng²	疼	pain, sore; kindly feeling, affection, love.
tien¹	癲	mad, madness; convulsions, fits.
ting¹	疔	a pimple, an ulcer, a venereal sore.
tou⁴	痘	the small-pox.
t'u¹	禿	itching of the head; a sore head.
t'ung⁴	痛	pain, painful, sore; acute feeling; wounded; very, extremely.
tz'ŭ¹	疵	disease; fault of temper, failing, fault.
wên¹	瘟	an epidemic.
ya³	瘂	dumb, dumbness; the back part of the neck.
yang³	痒	an itching sore; a scab; to itch, itching.
yang³	癢	same.
yao⁴	瘧	fever and ague.
yi⁴	疫	an epidemic, plague, pestilence, distemper. See i⁴.

yin³	癮	a rash, an eruption.
yü¹	瘀	chronic disease; local accumulation of blood, &c.
yung¹	癰	a swelling, a sore, an ulcer, an abscess.

105

po 癶

fa¹	發	to send; to issue forth; to spring up, to raise higher.
têng¹	登	to ascend, to place higher.

106

pai 白

chieh¹	皆	all, the whole of.
'hao⁴	皓	light, bright, white.
'huang²	皇	imperial, august, majestic.
pai²	白	white, clear, manifest, obvious; to explain; in vain. See po².
pai²	百	a hundred; many, numerous; all, the whole. See po².
po²	白	white. See pai².
po²	百	a hundred. See pai².
ti²	的	sign of the possessive; real, true; clear, bright; a target.
tsao⁴	皂	police runners; black.
tsao⁴	皁	same.

107
p'i 皮

chou⁴	皺	wrinkles in any thing; frowns.
p'i²	皮	skin, hide, bark, peel; a case, a wrapper; to skin.

108
min 皿

chan³	盞	a cup; Numerative of lamps, &c.
ch'êng²	盛	to put into; to contain or receive. See *sheng⁴*.
chien¹	監	to inspect, to oversee, to examine; a eunuch; a prison; to imprison.
chin⁴	盡	the extreme, the utmost; to exhaust, to empty.
chung¹	盅	a cup.
'ho²	盒	a small box; to cover over; a cover.
i²	益	to increase, to benefit; benefit, advantage. See *yi²*.
k'uei¹	盔	a helmet; general term for vessels.
mêng²	盟	an oath; to vow, to swear.
min³	皿	crockery, earthenware.
p'an²	盤	a vessel, a tub, a dish, a plate; coiled up.
pei¹	盃	a cup.
p'ên²	盆	a cup, basin, jar, pitcher, tub, &c.
shêng⁴	盛	abundant, plentiful, affluent; great. See *ch'êng²*.

t'ang⁴	盪	tossing about, unsteady, agitated; a bathing tub.
tao⁴	盜	to rob, to plunder, to pilfer, to steal.
yi²	益	addition, advantage; to add to, to increase, to benefit. See i².
ting²	盈	full, overflowing, excess, overplus.
yü²	盂	a cup, a basin, a plate.

109
mu 目

cha³	眨	to wink, to blink.
chên¹	眞	true, sincere, real, genuine, pure.
chên¹	真	same.
chên¹	瞋	to stare with anger or dislike.
chêng¹	睜	to open the eyes wide, to stare.
ch'iao²	瞧	to look, to see.
chih²	直	straight, direct, upright, correct, proper.
k'ih⁴	眵	blear-eyed, sore eyes.
ding¹	睛	the pupil of the eye.
c'ou³	瞅	to look, to see.
chian⁴	眷	affection for; a family; near relations.
chu⁴	矗	upright, straight; to raise; eminent.
hsü¹	瞎	blind, blindness; ignorance.

hsiang¹	相	mutual, reciprocal; with; to blend, to harmonize.
hsing³	省	to look carefully, to examine, to investigate, to enquire. See *shêng³*.
hsüan²	眩	shifting the eyes continually, looking furtively.
k'an⁴	看	to look, to see, to observe, to perceive.
k'uang⁴	眶	the hollow of the eye.
lêng⁴	睖	to stare at.
liao³	瞭	good eyesight, able to see to a distance distinctly.
man²	瞞	to blind, to deceive, to impose upon; dullness of sight.
mei²	眉	the eyebrows.
mei⁴	眛	dulness of sight, indistinctness of vision.
mêng¹	矇	dull, obscure, indistinct; blind, ignorant, unlearned.
mi¹	眯	blinded, obscured, closed; to dislike, to loathe; dust in the eye.
mien²	眠	to shut the eyes, to sleep; confused, bewildered, perturbed.
mu⁴	目	the eye; to name, to designate; the principal; the index.
mu⁴	睦	friendly, cordial, kind, true; attached to; to agree; agreement.
p'an⁴	盼	to hope, to expect, to look towards.
sa²	瞂	the eye to light on.
shêng³	省	a province; to lessen, to diminish; to save. See *hsing³*.
shui⁴	睡	to sleep.
shun¹	眉	a shield. Also *tun*.

têng⁴	瞪	to open the eyes wide, to stare.
tu¹	督	to direct, to administer, to rule, to govern; to reprove; to lead; to correct, to examine; all.
tu³	睹	to look, to see, to observe.
tun³	眈	to take a nap, to doze; affected sleep; dulness of sight.
t'ung²	瞳	the pupil of the eye; to stare, to gaze.
yen³	眼	the eye; Num. of wells.

110
mou 矛

ching¹	矜	to compassionate, to feel for; to regret, regretful.
mou²	矛	a spear.
wu⁴	務	business; must.
yü⁴	豫	undecided, irresolute.

111
shih 矢

ai³	矮	a dwarf; low, short.
chih¹	知	to know, to perceive; to cause to know, to tell.
chü⁴	矩	a square; a rule; law, usage; a pattern; correct.
i³	矣	final particle; affirmation.
shih²	矢	an arrow, a dart; straightforward; to vow, to swear.

tuan³	短	short, low; to shorten; to come short in one's duty; to be in fault.
ts'o²	矬	a dwarf; dwarfish, stunted.

112
shih 石

ai⁴	礙	to obstruct, to hinder, to interfere with.
ai⁴	碍	same.
ch'ên³	磣	sand mixed with any thing, gritty.
chi²	礩	stone steps, any steps; an impediment.
ch'i⁴	砌	to raise in layers, (as a wall.)
chieh²	碣	a stone tablet.
ch'ing⁴	磬	a musical stone used as a bell.
ch'üeh⁴	確	certainly, really, truly, in fact, assuredly.
chu¹	硃	vermilion, cinnabar.
chuan¹	磚	bricks, tiles or flags.
fan²	礬	alum.
'hang¹	硪	a rammer; to ram ground for building, &c.
hsiao¹	硝	saltpetre, nitre.
k'an³	砍	to cut, to chop, to fell.
k'o¹	磕	to knock, to bump.
kung³	礦	a mine.

lei³	磊	rocks or stones piled up.
liu²	硫	sulphur, brimstone.
lu³	磠	sand, pebbles, shingle.
lu⁴	磟	uneven; rocky, uneven ground; small.
ma³	碼	the carnelian; weights; a yard.
mo²	磨	to grind, to rub; to afflict; a stone, a mill.
nien³	碾	a stone roller (either for field or grain.)
p'ao⁴	礮	a cannon.
pei¹	碑	a stone tablet.
p'êng⁴	硑	to run against, to come in contact with.
pi⁴	碧	blue or green stone, jade, jasper.
p'i¹	砒	arsenic.
p'ing¹	砰	a noise, rumbling noise, as of stone falling, &c.
p'o⁴	破	to break, to crack, to tear; to ruin; found out; defeated.
sui⁴	碎	in fragments, tatters, broken, odd bits; miscellaneous articles.
sha¹	砂	sand, pebbles.
shih²	石	a stone, stones, rocks; a measure (300 catties.) See tan¹.
tan¹	石	a picul. See shih².
têng⁴	磴	stone steps, stairs; lofty, precipitous; a stone bridge.
tieh²	碟	plates, saucers.

to⁴	碌	to stamp the foot.
t'o⁴	砣	weights; a roller.
tui⁴	碓	a pestle; a mortar.
tz'ŭ²	磁	Chinaware, porcelain; loadstone.
wan³	碗	a basin, bowl or cup.
yen²	研	to rub Chinese ink on the ink-slab.
yen⁴	硯	an ink-slab; to rub.
ying⁴	硬	hard, stiff, firm, unbending, unyielding; powerful.

113
shih 示

ch'an³	禪	meditation, contemplation, abstraction.
chên¹	禎	a favorable prognostic.
chi⁴	祭	to sacrifice, to offer up.
ch'i²	祈	to pray, to supplicate, to call upon, to invoke.
ch'i²	祇	respect, awe, veneration.
chin⁴	禁	to forbid, to prohibit, to hinder, to ward off.
chu⁴	祝	praises, thanksgivings; to pray.
fu²	福	happiness, blessings, prosperity.
'hu⁴	祜	same.
'huo⁴	禍	evil, injury, misery, calamity, misfortune, adversity.

hsi³	禧	auspicious, felicitous, happy, blissful.
hsiang²	祥	an auspicious omen, good fortune.
li³	禮	rites, ceremonies; politeness; propriety, decorum, becoming; presents.
lu³	祿	blessedness, happiness; emoluments of office, official income.
p'i⁴	祕	secret, hidden, mysterious, abstruse.
p'iao⁴	票	a money order, a pawn-broker's ticket, a warrant, a signal; a beacon.
ping³	稟	to state to a superior; to receive; to give information; to petition; to confer; a statement.
sui⁴	祟	gambols, pranks, evil influences (of spirits.)
shê⁴	社	a deity; a sacrifice; an alter; a parish.
shên²	神	spirits, animal spirits; spiritual, divine; divinity; God.
shih⁴	示	a proclamation; to declare, to proclaim, to manifest; to admonish.
ssŭ⁴	祀	to sacrifice to gods or departed spirits.
tao³	禱	to pray, to entreat, to supplicate.
tsu³	祖	ancestors; a grand-father; to begin; beginning, origin.
tz'ŭ²	祠	temple of ancestors; to sacrifice.
yü⁴	禦	to oppose, to stop, to hinder.

114
jou 肉

ch'in²	禽	birds in general.

115
'ho 禾

ch'êng¹	稱	to weigh; to designate, to style as; to compliment, to praise.
ch'êng²	程	to travel; a road, a stage; a limit; a pattern.
ch'êng⁴	秤	balances, scales. See yao⁴.
chi¹	稽	to examine into, to compare; to bow.
chi²	積	to accumulate, to collect together, to hoard, to pile up.
chia⁴	稼	to sow, to plant.
chieh¹	秸	grain stalks; to husk grain.
ch'iu¹	秋	autumn.
ch'ou²	稠	thick, close together.
chung⁴	種	to plant or sow; seed, kind, class, sort; to beget.
'ho²	禾	crops in general.
'hui⁴	穢	dirt, filth, dirty, filthy, indecent, lewd; to debauch.
'hsi¹	稀	open, apart, few; careless, inattentive, remiss; thin, watery.
hsien¹	秈	a kind of rice.
hsiu⁴	秀	fine, elegant, fair, splendid, beautiful; shoots, sprouts.
i²	移	to remove, to change, to alter; to forward to.
jên⁴	稔	corn ears, ripe grain.
kao³	稿	straw; draft of a document, original copy.

kêng¹	秔	a kind of rice, common rice.
kêng¹	稉	same.
k'o¹	科	practice, profession; class, series; a rank; examination.
k'o¹	稞	wheat, grain.
ku³	穀	grain; real; solid, substantial; good; wealthy; continual succession.
lêng²	稜	grain; a neighbouring state; water chestnuts.
mu⁴	穆	grain; grandeur; respect; pleased, pleasant, cordial.
pai⁴	稗	tares; small, minute.
pei⁴	秕	grain that does not come to perfection, empty grain.
ping³	秉	to grasp, to hold up, to maintain; natural.
sê⁴	穡	to reap, to gather; saving, avaricious.
su¹	穌	to collect together; to desist, to rest; to revive; to enjoy; tranquil joy.
sui⁴	穗	ears of corn, flowers and fruits of grass.
shao¹	稍	the tip of a branch; in a small quantity, in a slight degree, rather, slightly; gradually.
shui¹	稅	revenue, taxes, duties; to bequeath.
ssŭ¹	私	private, selfish, interested, illicit, clandestine, individual; peculiar; plebian.
tao⁴	稻	rice, paddy.
t'u¹	秃	blunt, bald, bare.
tsu¹	租	to rent, to hire; a tax; grain paid as tax.
wên³	穩	firm, stable, safe; rest, repose.

yang¹	秧	grain thick and close; first shoots of grain.
yao⁴	秤	to weigh. See ch'êng⁴.

116
ˋ hsüeh 穴

chai³	窄	narrow, compressed, straitened.
chiao⁴	窖	a pit, a hole, a cavern, a cellar.
ch'iao⁴	竅	a hole, an aperture, an opening.
ch'ieh⁴	竊	clandestine, private; to steal; to investigate.
chih⁴	窒	to impede, to hamper, to embarrass.
chiu¹	究	to investigate, to scrutinize; finally, at last, after all.
chiung¹	窘	straitened, embarassed, pressed.
ch'iung²	穹	high, lofty; heaven; to stop up a hole.
ch'iung²	窮	to exhaust; extremity; impoverished, poor, poverty.
ch'uan¹	穿	to put on, to dress; to bore, to enter, to insert.
ch'uang¹	窗	a window. See 牕.
hsüeh⁴	穴	a hole, a den, a cave, a grave.
k'u¹	窟	a hole, a cave, a cavern, a rat hole.
k'uei²	窺	to peep, to spy, to look furtively.
k'ung¹	空	empty; to empty; vacant; great, wide; the firmament; abstraction; unprejudiced.
lung²	窿	a hole; the expanse or vault of heaven.

tiao⁴	窵	a bird's nest; deep; very.
t'u¹	突	to beat, to knock; to offend, to insult; to rush against; sudden, abrupt.
tsao⁴	竃	a furnace.
ts'uan⁴	竄	to burrow; to sneak off, to run away and hide; weak, petty; fearful.
wo¹	窩	a nest, den, cave, hole or lair.
yao²	窰	a kiln, a pottery.
yao³	窈	deep, profound; retired, still, tranquil.

117
li 立

chan⁴	站	to stand up; standing still, to stop; a stage of a journey.
chang¹	章	rules, regulations, laws; a section, a chapter; an essay; a composition.
chieh²	竭	to try to the utmost, the highest degree, extreme.
ching⁴	靖	to regulate; order, peace, tranquillity.
ching⁴	競	to strive, to wrangle; quarrelsome.
ching⁴	竟	then, at last, finally, after all, to the utmost.
chün⁴	竣	to complete, to finish, finished, completed, done.
li⁴	立	erect; to erect, to establish, to form, to fix, to arrange, to effect; soon, speedily.
sung²	竦	to shudder, the flesh creeping; horror, awe, fear, respect; to raise, to exalt.
shu⁴	竪	upright, perpendicular; to establish; a eunuch.

tuan¹	端	upright; to arrange; correct; the head; a beginning, a principle or cause; the end.
t'ung²	童	a boy, a lad; a girl, a virgin.

118

chu 竹

chên¹	箴	a probe; to probe; custom, rule.
chêng¹	箏	a kite; a musical instrument.
chi¹	箕	a star; a sieve or winnowing basket.
chi²	籍	a list, a book; the place one's ancestors belonged to.
chieh¹	節	a joint, a limit; a period of time; a feast day.
chien¹	箋	note paper. See 牋.
chien³	簡	to abridge, to diminish, to retrench; to survey.
ch'ien⁴	箭	an arrow.
ch'ien¹	籤	slips of wood used for drawing lots; a magistrate's warrant.
ch'ien¹	籖	same.
ch'ih²	笞	a bamboo stick; to beat, to chastise.
chin¹	筋	tendons, muscles; inclination; a catty.
chou³	箒	a broom; to sweep.
ch'ou²	籌	to calculate, to reckon, to plan; a tally.
chu²	築	to build mud walls or houses.
chu²	竹	the bamboo.

chu⁴	筋	chopsticks.
chu⁴	箸	same.
chuan⁴	篆	the seal character.
fa²	筏	a raft.
fan⁴	範	a mould, a pattern; a rule, usage or custom.
fu²	符	spells, charms; to agree or tally; deficient; a tally or check.
ʻhuang²	簧	a kind of flute, Pandean pipes.
hsiang¹	箱	a box, trunk or chest; a small room.
hsiao¹	簫	a kind of flageolet.
hsiao⁴	笑	to smile, to laugh; to ridicule; to be pleased.
kan¹	竿	a bamboo stick.
ko⁴	箇	a piece, a particle; Numerative of many things. See 個.
ku¹	箍	a hoop; to hoop.
kʻuai⁴	筷	chopsticks.
kuan³	管	a tube; reeds; to rule, to control; Num. of pens, &c.
kʻuang¹	筐	a basket.
lan²	籃	same (hand).
li⁴	籬	a hedge, a fence made with bamboo.
lien²	簾	a screen, a curtain.
lo²	籮	a bamboo basket for carrying things in on a pole.

lou³	簍	a bamboo basket, a hamper.
lung²	籠	a cage; a basket; to hoard up; to monopolize.
mi²	篾	bamboo skin; small.
pa¹	笆	a kind of bamboo; a fence.
pên⁴	笨	stupid, thick-headed; clumsy, coarse, unwieldy.
p'êng²	篷	a mat sail, any kind of sail or awning.
pi²	篦	a small-tooth comb.
pi³	筆	a pen, a pencil.
p'ien¹	篇	a page, a leaf, a section; a bamboo; a publication, a proclamation.
po⁴	簸	a wicker dustpan, a sort of winnowing basket.
pu⁴	簿	a memorandum book, an account book, a register.
suan⁴	算	to reckon, to calculate, to number; to speculate, to guess; speculation; to scheme.
sun³	筍	bamboo shoots.
sun³	笋	same.
shai¹	篩	a sieve, a strainer; to sift, to strain.
shai¹	簁	to sift.
shao¹	筲	a bucket.
shêng¹	笙	a musical instrument; pipes.
ta¹	答	to reply, to answer; to recompense; to sustain.
têng²	等	to wait; till class, grade, kind, quality, species or sort; plural of pronouns.

chu 竹	149	*mi* 米

t'êng²	籐	cane.
ti²	笛	a flute.
ti⁴	第	order, series; prefix which makes numbers ordinal; a literary degree; but; only.
t'iao²	篠	a broom; to sweep.
tu³	篤	true, real, genuine, pure; unmixed; thick; firm; strong; important; simple.
t'ung³	筒	a tube, a case, a hollow bamboo.
tsan¹	簪	flat hair-pins; a branch.
ts'ê⁴	策	a plan, a scheme, a stratagem; to scheme, to devise; a switch, a whip.
yen²	筵	a mat; a feast, banquet or entertainment.
yen²	簷	the eaves of a house.

119
mi 米

chan¹	粘	paste; to paste; adhesive; a supplement. See *nien²*.
chiang⁴	糨	flour and water, paste.
ching¹	精	pure, fine, spiritual; essence; semen; clear, bright.
ching¹	粳	rice produced on dry soil.
ch'iu³	糗	burnt, parched; parched wheat.
chou¹	粥	rice-water or gruel, congee.
chuang⁴	粧	a lady's toilet; dressed, ornamented, rouged, made up; to pretend.
fên³	粉	meal, flour, powder, paint; to whitewash.

*fên*³	糞	excrement, filth, manure, ordure.
ʻ*hu*²	糊	paste; to paste.
*kʻang*¹	糠	the husk of grain, chaff.
*kao*¹	糕	a kind of steamed pudding; a bait; gruel.
*la*¹	穬	the spikes of grain.
*li*⁴	粒	a grain of rice; food (particularly rice).
*li*⁴	糲	coarse food; the refuse of pounded rice.
*liang*²	糧	grain; a daily ration; pay of the soldiers; taxes.
*liang*²	粮	grain, corn, food generally.
*liang*²	粱	millet.
*mi*³	米	rice, seeds.
*mo*¹	糢	dimness, indistinct.
*nien*²	粘	paste; any glutinous substance; to paste. See *chan*¹.
*su*²	粟	maize, Indian corn; small sand.
*sui*⁴	粹	unmixed, pure, all the same; complete.
*tʻang*²	糖	sugar, candy, honey.
*ti*²	糴	to buy rice or grain; fleet, quick.
*tʻiao*⁴	糶	to sell grain.
*tsao*¹	糟	rotten; dregs, grains.
*tsʻu*¹	粗	large, open, coarse, vulgar, boisterous, indecent.

mi 米	151	*ssŭ* 糸

*tsung*⁴ 粽 three-cornered millet dumplings.

*yüeh*⁴ 粤 initial particle; in; to say; a name of Canton.

120
ssŭ 糸

*chan*⁴ 綻 a hole, a slit, a rent, a seam opened; to open.

*ch'an*² 纏 to wind round, to bind, to tie, to wrap up.

*chi*¹ 績 to wind silk; meritorious deeds, business, affairs, work done.

*chi*² 級 series, steps or degrees; a grade; classed, sorted.

*chi*⁴ 紀 to record; to arrange and number; age.

*chi*⁴ 繫 a line of succession, successively, hereditary.

*chi*⁴ 繼 to connect; related to; to tie, to bind or fasten: See *hsi*⁴.

*chi*⁴ 緝 to pursue closely; to seize; to bind.

*chiang*¹ 繮 a bridle.

*chiang*⁴ 絳 a deep red, crimson.

*chiao*³ 絞 to wrap round and twist, to strangle.

*chiao*³ 繳 to return to, to pay to, to hand in, to deliver up.

*chieh*² 結 to tie; a knot; fixed, formed; to contract, to bind; a bond; to bear.

*chien*³ 繭 the cocoon of the silkworm.

*ch'ien*¹ 縴 to unravel; a tow-rope; to pull, to drag, to lead.

*chih*¹ 織 to weave.

chih³	紙	paper.
chih⁴	緻	fine, delicate, soft, elegant, effeminate.
chin³	緊	tight, compressed, pressing, urgent, strict.
ching¹	經	past; religious and classical books; to superintend; the menses.
ch'o⁴	綽	slow, leisurely; wide, roomy, extensive.
chou⁴	縐	a kind of crape; rumpled.
ch'ou²	紬	woven silk.
ch'ou²	綢	same.
chüan⁴	絹	lutestring; a handkerchief, a napkin.
chüeh²	絕	cut off, broken off, interrupted, terminated.
ch'un²	純	silk thread; pure, genuine, unmixed, honest. See *shun²*.
chung¹	終	the end, the close, finis; to end, to terminate, to die; the whole.
fan¹	繙	to translate; to turn over.
fan²	繁	numerous; multifarious; confused.
fang³	紡	to make thread, to spin, to twist.
fên¹	紛	perplexed, confused; hurry, bustle; many, numerous.
fêng²	縫	to sew; a seam, an opening, crack or fissure.
fu²	縛	to tie, to bind fast.
'huan³	緩	slow, dilatory; careless; to delay, to postpone.
'hui⁴	繪	to sketch or paint pictures; to embellish, to adorn.

'hung²	紅	red; to hope, to expect, to anticipate; good.
hsi⁴	系	to connect, connected; relation to; belonging to; is, am.
hsi⁴	細	fine, small, minute, petty, trifling; delicate; careful; distinct.
hsi⁴	繋	to connect, connected; in succession; related to; to tie, to bind. See chi⁴. _kind with_
hsien²	絃	string of a musical instrument.
hsien⁴	綫	thread; a clue, a trace; a spy; a fuze.
hsien⁴	線	same.
hsien⁴	縣	a district fifth in order; principal town of a district; a magistrate.
hsiu⁴	綉	to embroider; embroidery.
hsiu⁴	繡	same.
hsü⁴	緒	the commencement, the beginning.
hsü⁴	續	to connect; continuous, a continuation, a supplement.
hsü⁴	絮	gossamer, willow down; prolix, talkative.
i⁴	縊	to strangle, to hang one's self.
i⁴	繹	the utmost; unceasingly, uninterruptedly; to unravel.
jao⁴	繞	to wind silk. Same as 遶.
jung²	絨	velvet, cloth, worsted, flannel, coarse silk.
kang¹	綱	the large cord of a net; to regulate, to control.
kao³	縞	plain, white, unadorned; plain white silk.
kei³	給	to give; to, for.

k'un³	綑	to weave.
lan²	攬	a rope, a cable; to tie; to drag.
lao⁴	絡	a net; silk or hemp thread. See lo⁴.
lei³	累	to implicate, to trouble, to embarrass; to heap upon, to pile up.
lien²	縺	connected fast together; indissoluble.
lien⁴	練	to select, to choose; to experiment, to learn by experience.
ling²	綾	a fine sort of silk, damask silk.
liu³	綹	one hundred silk threads; a strand, a lock, a tress.
lo⁴	絡	a net; silk or hemp fibres; the blood vessels. See lao⁴.
lü³	縷	silk thread.
lü⁴	綠	green. See lu⁴.
lün²	綸	to wind silk; to classify, to adjust, to put in order. See lun².
lu⁴	綠	green. See lü⁴.
lun²	綸	to wind silk; to classify, to adjust. See lün².
mien²	綿	cotton; floss silk; connected; enduring; thick, close; weak.
na⁴	納	within; to put into; to give; to receive, to take.
pan⁴	絆	a loop, a sort of lasso; to trip up.
pang³	綁	to tie, to bind.
pang³	縍	to bind shoes; shoe-binding.
pêng¹	繃	to tie, to bind, to fasten, to tighten.

pêng¹	繃	same.
pien¹	編	to weave, to fabricate, to twist, to plait; to compose, to arrange; to connect.
so¹	縮	to collapse, to draw in, to contract, to pucker up, to shrink.
so³	索	to drag, to extort; to bind; string, cord; binding; a law.
su⁴	素	white, plain, simple, unadorned; the original state of; heretofore.
sui¹	綏	traces of a carriage; steady, tranquil, quiet.
sui³	繐	tassels, fringes.
sha¹	紗	crape, gauze.
shao⁴	紹	to connect, to join; to continue in succession; to lead.
shên¹	紳	a sash, a girdle; to girt; gentry.
shêng²	繩	string, cord, rope; to warn; to restrict, to restrain.
shun²	純	silk thread; pure, unmixed; ripe; acquainted; great. See ch'un².
ssŭ¹	絲	silk, raw silk; small, minute; fine as silk; a weight.
tuan⁴	緞	satin.
t'ung³	統	a head, a leader; the origin, beginning; end of a clue; the whole, entire; general.
tsa¹	紮	to tie round, to tie, to bind.
ts'ai²	纔	just, just now, but a moment ago; scarcely; then; it will then.
ts'ai³	綵	coloured silk.
tsu³	組	fringe, silken cords, tassels; a stamp.
tsuan³	纂	women's back hair; to collect, to arrange.

tsung³	總	to collect; collectively, all, the whole; general; a bundle; a sheaf.
tsung⁴	縱	to loosen, to let go; to tolerate, to allow; although, though; remiss, disorderly.
tzŭ³	紫	purple, a dark brown; imperial.
wang³	網	a net, a web.
wei²	維	to tie, to bind, to connect; to help.
wei⁴	緯	to weave, to bind; to fasten; the woof; tassels.
wên²	紋	streaks; fine silk.
yi⁴	繹	to arrange; to state; to explain; to end; to fill. See i⁴.
yo²	約	to bind, to restrain, to contract; a contract, an agreement, a treaty.
yüan²	緣	origin, clue, cause; a border, selvage or hem.
yün²	紜	numbers thrown into confusion, ravelled, tangled.

121

fou 缶

ch'ing⁴	罄	an empty jar; exhausted; a kind of bell.
ch'üeh¹	缺	a deficiency, a want; to vacate; a vacancy.
fou³	缶	a jar, a basin, crockery.
kang¹	缸	a large earthenware vessel, a vat.
kuan⁴	罐	a jar, a jug, a mug; a tea cannister.
t'an²	罎	a wine bottle.
tsun⁴	罇	a pan, a vat, a bottle.

122
wang 网

chao⁴	罩	a cover; a shade; to cover; to shade.
chih⁴	置	to purchase; to place, to appoint.
fa²	罰	to punish; punishment; a fine; to fine, to censure; an offence.
'han³	罕	rare, scarce, few, unfrequent.
kua⁴	罣	to hook on to; to fall into a net; to rush against; an impediment.
lo²	羅	a net; a sort of silk; to arrange in order.
ma⁴	罵	to rail, to abuse, to scold, to use opprobrious language.
pa⁴	罷	to desist, to stop; to say nothing more about; a final sound.
shu⁴	署	a public office; acting temporarily; to be attached to; the 8th month.
tsui⁴	罪	crimes, offences; punishment; to criminate.
wang³	罔	a net; confounded; stopped; not, without; to impose upon.

123
yang 羊

ch'ün²	羣	a flock, a herd, a crowd; comrades, companions, friends.
ch'ün²	群	same.
hsi¹	羲	name of the founder of the Chinese monarchy.
hsien⁴	羨	to covet, to desire; to praise, to admire; excess, overplus.
hsiu¹	羞	shame; ashamed; to blush.

i⁴	義	good, right, proper, disinterested, righteous; righteousness, justice.
kao¹	羔	a lamb, a kid.
kêng¹	羹	broth, soup.
mei³	美	handsome, beautiful, elegant, fine, becoming, sweet, good, excellent.
shan¹	羶	smell of animals; rank, frouzy, fetid.
yang²	羊	the sheep.

124
yü 羽

ch'ih⁴	翅	wings, fins.
fan¹	翻	to fly backward and forwards; to turn over, to upset.
fei³	翡	green; a kind of kingfisher.
'han⁴	翰	a pencil.
hsi²	習	to practise, to accustom; to repeat; custom, habit.
i¹	翳	the film or skin over the eye; to cover, to hide; to screen, a fan.
i⁴	翼	wings; the flanks; to assist; an assistant. See yi⁴.
ling²	翎	wings, feathers, peacocks' feathers.
ts'ui⁴	翠	blue; the kingfisher.
wêng¹	翁	an old man; a title of respect.
yao⁴	耀	splendour; bright, glorious; to dazzle.

yi⁴	翼	wings (literally or figuratively). See i⁴.
yü³	羽	feathers, wings.

125
lao 老

chê²	者	this, he, she, it, they, who.
cho²	者	same.
k'ao³	考	aged; to examine, to compare, to interrogate.
lao³	老	old, aged, venerable; a term of honour and respect.

126
êrh 而

chuan¹	耑	the origin or source; singly, solely, special.
êrh²	而	and, as, but, on the contrary.
nai⁴	耐	patient, to bear, to endure; to forbear; patient endurance.
shua²	耍	to play, to trifle, to amuse; to fence; to gamble.

127
lei 耒

ch'u²	耡	to cultivate; agriculture, husbandry; to assist.
'hao⁴	耗	to lessen; to waste; to spoil, to injure; a rat or mouse.
kêng¹	耕	to till, to plough, to cultivate.
lei³	耒	a plough.

nou⁴	耨	to hoe; a hoe; to weed; to dress a field.
p'a²	耙	a rake or harrow; to rake.
p'a²	耙	same.
yün²	耘	to weed; to remove.

128
êrh 耳

chih²	職	to direct, to control, to manage; office; an officer.
ch'ih³	耻	shame, ashamed.
chü⁴	聚	to assemble, to collect; an assemblage.
êrh³	耳	the ear; handles of a box, &c.
kêng³	耿	bright; straightforward, resolute, determined.
liao²	聊	carelessly, anyhow; a desire or wish; to depend upon.
lien²	聯	to join, to connect, to unite; to arrange; connected with; associated together.
lung²	聾	deaf, deafness.
p'in⁴	聘	to request, to ask, to enquire; to betroth, to espouse; betrothal; marriage presents.
shêng¹	聲	sound, noise, tone, voice; to speak, to state; to praise.
shêng⁴	聖	sacred, sainted, holy, canonized, virtuous, wise; a sage.
ta¹	耷	pendant, to hang down; large ears.
tan¹	耽	to loiter, to delay; large pendant ears; excessive indulgence.
t'ing¹	聽	to hear, to listen; to comply, to obey; to wait.

tsung⁴	聳	quiet; to jump; to excite, to stimulate; to elevate; to hear; deaf.
ts'ung¹	聰	quickness of apprehension, perception or hearing.
yeh²	耶	father; interrogative particle.

129
yü 聿

'hua⁴	畫	to draw or paint; a picture.
i⁴	肆	practised in, versed in, well acquainted with.
su⁴	肅	dread, fear, awe, respect, reverence; courteous; to respect; to recede.

130
jou 肉

chang⁴	脹	swelling of the stomach.
ch'ang²	腸	the intestines, the bowels.
chi¹	肌	the human flesh, the body.
chi³	脊	the spine; the ridge of a mountain; the back of anything.
ch'i²	臍	the navel.
ch'iang¹	腔	puffed up with wind; vain, empty, conceited.
chiao¹	膠	glue; to glue; adherence to.
chiao³	脚	the foot.
chiao³	腳	same.
chien¹	肩	the shoulders; to sustain.

L

chih¹	脂	grease, fat, lard, cosmetic.
chih¹	肢	the limbs.
chou³	肘	the elbow.
chou⁴	胄	a helmet, a casque; descendants, posterity; long after.
ch'un²	脣	the lips.
chung³	腫	to swell; a swelling; inflated, puffed up.
fei²	肥	fat, fleshy; rich, affluent, plentiful.
fei⁴	肺	the lungs; mysterious, secret.
fu²	腹	the bowels; trusted friends.
fu³	脯	dried meat.
fu³	腑	the viscera, the bowels.
fu³	腐	rotten, corrupted, corruption.
fu⁴	膚	to receive; the skin.
'hu²	胡	blindly, wildly, recklessly; a street or lane.
hsiao⁴	肖	to imitate, to follow in the footsteps or ways of, &c.
hsing¹	腥	raw meat; unpleasant smell, stinking.
hsiu¹	脩	dried meat; the salary of teachers, &c.
hsiung¹	胷	the breast.
hsiung¹	胸	same.
hsü¹	胥	inferior clerks, runners, &c.

i²	胰	soap.
jou⁴	肉	meat, flesh.
kan¹	肝	the liver.
kang¹	肛	the rectum, the anus.
kao¹	膏	fat, lard; greasy; rich food; a plaster.
k'ên³	肯	to wish, to be willing, to choose to, to permit.
ko¹	肐	the elbow.
ko²	胳	the armpit.
ko²	膈	the breast, the chest.
ku³	股	the thighs; a division, a body, a gang or band.
k'ua⁴	胯	legs or thighs; space between the thighs.
kuan³	脘	the stomach.
kuang²	胱	the bladder.
lei⁴	肋	the ribs, the sides.
lieh⁴	肋	the ribs.
lien²	臁	the sides of the legs.
lien³	臉	the cheek, the face, the countenance; reputation.
lü³	膂	the spine, the backbone.
lu²	臚	the skin; arranged in order; to report.
lung²	朧	confused; drowsy; fat.

mang²	肓	severe illness; the thorax; indistinctness of vision.
mo⁴	脈	the pulse, veins, arteries; streaks; the blood flowing.
mo⁴	膜	to soothe, to touch delicately; the inner skin or peel.
nao³	腦	brains; glossy, soft.
nêng²	能	able to, competent to, can; ability, power, talent.
nêng²	膿	matter, corruption, pus.
ni⁴	膩	fat, glossy, smooth, oily; congealed; only.
p'ang¹	胖	stout, fleshy, fat, large; ugly.
p'ang⁴	膀	the bladder.
p'ang⁴	胖	stout, fleshy, large, fat; a slice of; enjoying ease. See p'ang¹.
pao¹	胞	the womb.
pei⁴	臂	the fore-arm, the arm in general.
pei⁴	背	the back; to carry on the back; to turn the back upon; to oppose; behind the back.
p'ei¹	胚	an unformed mass, an embryo; clouds, vapour. See p'i¹.
p'êng²	膨	a swelling of the stomach, swollen, bloated.
p'i¹	胚	sort, kind. See p'ei¹.
p'i²	脾	the spleen.
piao¹	臕	sleek and stout, fat.
po²	脖	the neck.
po⁴	膊	the arm; dried meat; a large slice.

sai¹	腮	the jaws, the side of the face.
sao⁴	臊	ashamed; fat, lard, raw meat.
shan⁴	膳	the Emperor's meals; good cuisine.
shên⁴	腎	the kidneys; the genitals, the testicles; to lead, to induce.
t'ai¹	胎	the womb; pregnancy; a conception, a fœtus.
tan³	胆	the gall; courage.
tan³	膽	same.
t'ang²	膛	the centre of the breast.
t'ien³	腆	thick, substantial; abundant; large; good; many, much.
t'o¹	脫	to take off or away, to put off; to retire, to avoid, to escape; to fade; to be born.
tu³	肚	the entrails, the stomach, the belly.
t'ui³	腿	the legs, the thighs.
tsang⁴	臟	the bowels; the kidneys; to cherish.
ts'ang¹	臢	dirty.
ts'ui⁴	脆	gristle, cartilage; brittle.
wan⁴	腕	the wrist; to turn, to twist.
wei⁴	胃	the intestines.
yao¹	腰	the loins, the waist.
yeh⁴	腋	the armpit.
yen¹	胭	the throat; rouge.

ying¹	膺	the breast; near; related to; to receive; to sustain; a girth.
yü⁴	育	to bear, to rear, to bring up, to nourish, to educate.

131
ch'ên 臣

ch'ên²	臣	a minister, a statesman, a public servant.
lin²	臨	to descend, to approach; about to, at the point of; to commence; large, great.
tsang¹	臧	good, virtuous, faithful, generous.
wo⁴	臥	to recline, to lie down, to sleep, to rest, to cease.

132
tzŭ 自

nieh⁴	臬	a target, a door-post; a rule, a law; a judge.
tzŭ³	自	self, one's self; from.

133
chih 至

chih⁴	至	to arrive at, to, till; as to, respecting; the extreme.
chih⁴	致	to go to; to come to; to tend to; the cause; to exert.
t'ai²	臺	a terrace, a stage, a gallery.

134
chiu 臼

chiu⁴	臼	a mortar.
chiu⁴	舅	a maternal uncle.
chiu⁴	舊	old (applied to time, persons, place or things); a long time.
chü³	舉	to lift up or raise, to elevate; to introduce, to recommend.
hsing¹	興	to arise, to get up; to allow; to delight in; flourishing.
wai³	舀	to bale (as water, &c.); a ladle.
yao³	舀	same.
yü²	臾	a moment, an instant.
yu³	與	with, to, from, by, and; to use, to employ; good.

135
shê 舌

kuan³	館	tea or eating houses, an inn; a hall; a school; an establishment.
p'u³	舖	a shop; to spread, to arrange, to extend. See 鋪.
shê²	舌	the tongue, tongue of a bell, buckle, &c.
shê⁴	舍	a cottage, a shed; to stop, to rest, to lodge; my; junior relations.
shu¹	舒	open, unrolled; to open, to expand, to exhilirate; ease, comfort, order.
t'ien³	舔	to lick. See 餂.
t'ien³	舚	to put out the tongue.

136
ch'uan 舛

ch'uan³ 舛 error, erroneous; to contradict.

shun⁴ 舜 name of a celebrated emperor; benevolent; sage.

wu³ 舞 to gesticulate, to posture, to dance; to fence; sleight of hand.

137
chou 舟

chou¹ 舟 a boat.

ch'uan² 船 a boat or vessel of any kind.

pan¹ 般 manner, way, fashion; class, sort; to revert to; to divide; to distribute.

pang³ 榜 to board a vessel; two vessels side by side.

t'ing³ 艇 a boat, a barge.

to⁴ 舵 a helm, a rudder.

ts'ang¹ 艙 the hold of a vessel.

138
kén 艮

chien¹ 艱 difficult, distressing, dangerous.

kén⁴ 艮 perverse.

liang² 良 good, virtuous; to be able to do.

139
sê 色

sê⁴	色	colour; quality, description, kind, manner, appearance; lust, sexual pleasure.
shai³	色	same.

140
tsao 艸

ch'a²	茶	tea.
ch'ang¹	菖	a water plant used for making paper, a rush.
chao²	著	to become; to shew, to manifest; to cause; to take effect. See cho². *to put on clothing*
chêng¹	蒸	hot vapour, steam; to steam, to boil. *to wear*.
chia²	葭	reeds, rushes.
chiang¹	薑	ginger.
chiang¹	薑	same.
chiao¹	蕉	the plantain; the palm.
ch'iao²	蕎	a kind of rye. *buckwheat.*
chieh⁴	芥	mustard.
ch'ieh²	茄	the brinjal, the egg plant.
chien⁴	荐	to introduce, to recommend.
chien⁴	薦	same.
ch'ien⁴	茜	name of a plant used for dyeing red.

chih¹	芝	sesamum; hemp.
ch'in²	芹	celery, parsley.
ching¹	荆	a kind of thorny bush.
cho²	著	to order, to command; shews, the action of verbs; it is so, yes. See *chao²*.
chü²	菊	the chrysanthemum.
ch'u²	芻	the young of any birds; grass, hay.
chuang¹	莊	farm houses; plants growing; sedate, grave.
fan²	藩	a boundary, a frontier.
fan⁴	范	grass, herbage.
fang¹	芳	fragrant plants; fragrant, agreeable, pleasing, excellent.
fei³	菲	deficient, scanty, sparing in food, fasting.
fên¹	芬	the fragrance of flowers, herbs, &c.
fu²	芙	hibiscus mutabilis.
fu²	茯	China root.
'hao¹	蒿	asparagus; tansy; worthless, of no account.
'ho²	荷	the lotus or water lily; to bear, to sustain.
'hu²	葫	a pumpkin or gourd.
'hua¹	花	flowers; dissipation, pleasure; indistinct vision; to spend.
'hua²	華	flowers; elegant, brilliant, variegated; a name of China.
'huang¹	荒	wild, barren; a wilderness; drought, dearth, famine.

'hui⁴	蕙	a fragrant plant; a species of epidendrum.
'hun¹	葷	meat diet, strong savoured food.
hsi²	蓆	a mat.
hsiao¹	蕭	reduced, impoverished, indigent, &c.
hsien⁴	莧	spinach.
hsin¹	薪	fuel, firewood,
hsün⁴	蕈	fragrance of flowers.
i⁴	藝	profession, business, trade, art, science; ability; to plant.
jê³	惹	to stimulate, to excite, to provoke, to induce.
jo⁴	若	if, as.
jui³	蕊	petals, centre of a flower.
jui³	蘂	same.
jui³	蕋	same.
jung²	蓉	Hibicus mutabilis; African marigold.
jung²	茸	tinder; horn; thick, confused.
kai⁴	蓋	a cover; to cover, to screen; to build.
kai⁴	葢	same.
kêng³	莖	the stem of plants, flowers, &c.
ko²	葛	creeping plants.
kou³	苟	hurried, precipitate; to catch.

k'ou⁴	蔲	the nutmeg.
ku¹	苽	a gourd, pumpkin or melon.
k'u³	苦	bitter; unpleasant, distressing; painstaking; earnest, urgent; to dislike.
k'uei²	葵	the mallow, the sunflower.
kuo³	菓	fruit; really, truly (used for 果 also.)
la⁴	落	to leave out or behind; to put down. See lao⁴ and lo⁴.
lai²	莱	name of a plant.
lan²	蘭	the epidendrum.
lan²	藍	blue.
lao⁴	落	to sink, to fall, to settle, to set. See la⁴ and lao⁴.
li⁴	莉	name of a plant, and of a flower.
li⁴	荔	a kind of rush for making brooms of; a fragrant plant.
li⁴	藜	a stem, branch, fork or prong; a plant.
lien²	蓮	the lotus or water lily.
ling²	菱	the water chestnut.
ling²	苓	China root.
lo²	蘿	the turnip; a sort of creeper; to entwine; moss.
lo⁴	落	to let fall, to fall, to drop. See lao⁴ and la⁴.
lu²	蘆	a kind of reeds.
ma²	蔴	hemp.

mang²	芒	sharp point or beard of grain; a sharp point.
mang⁸	茫	uncertainty, vagueness, doubt; vastness.
mang³	莽	brushwood, jungle; tangled, disorderly, confused, indistinct.
mao²	茅	reeds, rushes; a water-closet.
mao⁴	茂	umbrageous, luxuriant, flourishing, strong, healthy.
mêng²	蒙	gloomy, dark, dull, obscure, blind; rash, rude; to receive; thankful.
mêng²	萌	plants budding, to bud, to germinate.
miao²	苗	sprouts, shoots, first budding of any plant.
miao³	藐	small, minute; petty, trifling, contemptuous, insignificant.
ming²	茗	tea of any sort.
mo²	蘑	the mushroom.
mo⁴	茉	the jessamine.
mo⁴	莫	no, not, do not, negative; a cessation of.
ou³	藕	the lotus or water-lily root.
pa¹	芭	a fence; musa coccinea.
pao²	薄	thin, light, slight, poor, bad; few, rare, single. See *po²*.
pêng²	蓬	a kind of flag; disorder, confused; luxuriant, growing freely.
p'ing²	萍	a sort of water lichen or moss.
p'ing²	蘋	the apple.
po¹	菠	cabbage; fruit.

po¹	蔔	turnips.
po²	薄	near, stingy; contemptuous; to browbeat; peppermint. See *pao²*.
p'u²	蒲	grapes.
p'u²	蘠	rushes of which mats are made.
sa⁴	薩	to assist, to help.
su¹	蘇	plentiful; cheerful, joyous, happy; to desist; to agitate; to revive.
su¹	蔬	vegetable food; a grain.
suan⁴	蒜	garlic.
sui⁴	荽	caraway, coriander.
shao²	芍	a medicine, an herb.
shên¹	蕣	a straw mat to sleep on when mourning for a parent.
shu³	薯	a sort of potato or yam.
shu³	菽	general term for pulse.
t'ai¹	苔	moss, lichens.
tang⁴	蕩	unsettled, agitated; spoiled.
t'ao²	萄	the grape.
t'êng²	藤	cane, vines, creepers.
t'i⁴	薙	to clear ground by burning off the grass, &c.
tou⁴	荳	pulse; the nutmeg.
tung³	董	to manage, to correct, to rule.

ts'ai⁴	菜	vegetables, victuals in general.
tsang⁴	葬	to inter, to bury.
ts'ang¹	蒼	azure; dark; old.
ts'ang²	藏	to hide, to conceal; to lay by, to store up; a receptacle.
ts'ao³	草	grass, weeds, straw; running hand; careless, heedless.
ts'ui⁴	萃	a kind of reed; to collect together.
ts'ung¹	葱	onions.
tz'ŭ²	茨	duckweed; to thatch; to collect.
tz'ŭ⁴	茦	thorns, prickles.
wan⁴	萬	ten thousand; an indefinitely large number; a superlative particle.
wei³	葦	reeds.
wei³	萎	plants drooping; diseased; contracted; rotten.
ya²	芽	shoots, sprouts, germs, buds; to bud; to begin.
yao⁴	葯	medicine; to heal.
yao⁴	藥	same.
yeh⁴	葉	leaf of a tree, book, &c.
yen¹	菸	tobacco. See 烟 and 煙.
yin⁴	蔭	shade cast by trees; umbrageous; to overshadow; shady.
ying¹	英	brave, gallant, heroic; talented; excellent, luxuriant, flourishing; flowers, foliage.
yü⁴	芋	a species of potato, taro.

yüan⁴	茻	grass, pasture; delicate, soft, luxuriant.
yün²	芸	a kind of bean; budding of plants; fragrant herbs.

141

‘hu 虍

ch‘ien²	虔	firm, determined; sincere; respectful, devout.
ch‘u³	處	a place; a circumstance; to stop, to rest; to manage.
‘hao⁴	號	a sign, a signal; a name, term or designation; to weep.
‘hu³	虎	the tiger.
hsü¹	虛	empty, void, vacant, vain, vacancy.
k‘uei¹	虧	to fail, to lose, to lessen, to injure; defect, failure, deficiency.
nio⁴	虐	tyrannical, unfeeling, harsh, fierce, cruel; to oppress; calamity.

142

ch‘ung 虫

cha³	鮓	name of a fish; an insect; fly-blown.
chê¹	蜇	to sting.
ch‘iang¹	蜣	a kind of beetle, a cockroach.
chiao¹	蛟	the crocodile.
chih¹	蜘	the spider.
ch‘ü¹	蛆	worms, maggots.

¹	蛐	worms; crickets.
ın³	綢	to lay by, to put aside, to remit.
	蛛	the spider.
	蛀	a kind of book-worm.
n³	蠢	simple, foolish, stupid, doltish.
ıg¹	螽	a kind of locust or grasshopper.
ıng²	蟲	general term for insects and reptiles.
ıng²	虫	same.
¹	蜂	a bee or wasp.
	蚨	an insect; copper money.
	蝠	a flying rat or squirrel, a bat.
'	蝦	the frog. See hsia¹.
'	蝴	the butterfly.
ıng²	蝗	the locust.
⁴	蟋	a kind of cricket or locust.
	蟀	the fighting cricket.
¹	蝦	crabs, prawns, shrimps, lobsters. See ha².
h¹	蝎	the scorpion.
h⁴	蟹	the crab.
	蟻	the ant.

kang⁴	虹	the rainbow.
ko²	蛤	cockles, clams, oysters, mussels.
kung¹	蚣	the centipede.
kuo¹	蟈	a sort of locust or grasshopper.
la⁴	蠟	wax, beeswax; waxed; a sort of resin.
lang²	螂	the beetle.
lo²	螺	a kind of periwinkle or whilk.
ma¹	蟆	the frog.
ma³	螞	the leech; the ant.
man³	蠻	rude, barbarous, unreasonable; barbarians.
mang³	蟒	the boa-constrictor.
mêng³	蠓	a kind of gnat.
mi⁴	蜜	honey; sweet; flattering.
o²	蛾	the moth.
pang⁴	蚌	oysters. See *pêng*.³
pang⁴	蜯	same.
p'ang²	螃	crabs.
pêng³	蚌	oysters. See *pang*⁴.
pien¹	蝙	a species of bat.
shê²	蛇	a snake, a serpent.

shih¹	蜦	cockles, whilks, periwinkles. See *ssŭ*¹.
shih¹	虱	a louse, lice.
shih²	蝕	to injure; to corrode; to diminish; to eclipse; an eclipse; to encroach.
shuai⁴	蟀	the cricket.
ssŭ¹	蜦	a cockle, a whilk; a screw. See *shih*¹.
tan⁴	蛋	eggs of any kind.
t'ang¹	螳	a kind of locust.
tieh²	蝶	a butterfly.
tu⁴	蠹	book-worms.
ts'an²	蠶	the silk worm.
tsao²	蚤	fleas (used also for *tsao*³ 早).
tz'ŭ⁴	蝍	a kind of grub.
wei⁴	蝟	the porcupine, the hedgehog.
wên²	蚊	the mosquito; gnats.
wu²	蜈	the centipede.
yin³	蚓	a worm.
ying¹	蠅	the fly.
ying²	螢	the firefly.
yu²	蝣	a kind of gnat; a grub.

143
hsieh 血

chung² 衆 all, the whole of, every; many, a multitude.
hsieh³ 血 blood.
hsüeh⁴ 血 same.
mo⁴ 脈 the pulse, veins, arteries; streaks; the blood flowing. See 脈.
niu⁴ 衄 to bleed at the nose; to wound with sharp weapons.

144
hsing 行

chieh¹ 街 a street.
ch'ung¹ 衝 a pathway, a thoroughfare; to rush against.
'hang² 行 a class, kind, sort or series; a row, a rank; a mercantile house; a firm.
'hu² 衚 a lane or street.
hsing² 行 to walk, to go; to do, to act; to allow; the conduct, the actions.
shu⁴ 術 path, road, method, way, device, artifice, scheme, trick, plan.
t'ung⁴ 衕 a street, a lane.
wei¹ 衛 to escort, to protect; an unwalled town; a military station.
ya² 衙 a bureau, a public office, a civil or military court.
yung³ 衖 a lane or street.

145
i 衣

ao^3	襖	a quilted coat; an overcoat.
$chih^4$	製	to make, to form; to compound; to decide, to regulate.
$chin^1$	襟	the overlap of a coat.
$ch'in^2$	衾	a coverlet; a shroud, a pall.
$ch'iu^3$	裘	fur clothing.
$ch'ün^2$	裙	a short skirt worn by women, a petticoat.
$chuang^1$	裝	to put into; to pack; to contain; to dress smartly, tastily.
$chung^1$	衷	justice, equity, fairness; just, right.
fu^2	袱	a wrapper; a bundle.
fu^4	複	lined or double clothes; double; to repeat.
$'ho^2$	褐	coarse woollen cloth, an outer garment; plush.
hsi^2	襲	in succession; to inherit; hereditary; to receive.
$hsieh^4$	褻	rags; to defile.
$hsiu^4$	袖	a sleeve, a cuff.
i^1	衣	clothes; a cover, a cloak, case, shell or skin.
i^1	裔	descendants, posterity.
ju^4	褥	a mattress; a mat.
$k'u^4$	褲	trousers, pantaloons, drawers.

k'u⁴	袴	same.
kua⁴	袿	an outer coat.
kuo³	裹	to swathe, to bandage; to bundle up; a bundle; a room, a recess.
lan²	襤	ragged, tattered; a single coverlet.
li³	裡	the inside of anything, in, within.
li³	裏	same.
lieh⁴	裂	to tear, to split, to crack; remnants of cloth, &c.
lo³	裸	naked.
lü⁴	褸	folds, pleats; ragged, tattered clothes.
na⁴	衲	a robe of the Buddhist priests.
p'an⁴	襻	a loop, a catch; a sash, a band.
pao¹	襃	to praise, to commend; large garments.
p'ao²	袍	a long outer garment.
pei⁴	裨	to give to, to assist, to supply; to benefit; to enable to do, to permit; small.
pei⁴	被	to endure, to bear, to suffer; to cover; a coverlet; to add to; to prepare. *by.*
piao³	表	a watch; to shew; a statement; the outside; relation by the mother's side.
piao³	裱	to paste; a kerchief.
pu³	補	to mend, to patch, to repair; to add on; to fill up; to make; to assist; to benefit.
shan¹	衫	a shirt or shift.
shang¹	裳	clothes; to screen off; a petticoat.

i^i	褱	to wear out; decay, decayed, worn out.
	褚	a bag, a wallet, a purse.
	袋	a bag, a purse; a sash; a cover for books.
^{3}	袒	to embrace, to enfold; a fold, a pleat; to expose a part of the body.
i^4	裭	to undress; the hands in the sleeves.
i^2	裁	to cut out (as a tailor); to cut off, to diminish; to conjecture.
i^1	襯	inner clothes; to assist; to confer, to give. Also ch'ên.
	襪	stockings.
	裕	liberal, generous, indulgent; affluent, plenty.

146
hsi 西

	覆	backwards and forwards; to subvert; to examine.
	覈	to examine, to investigate; to verify.
	西	the west; European.
^{1}	要	to want, to desire, to require; to be about to; requisite, important; if.

147
chien 見

o^4	覺	to awaken, to be aroused, to attend to, to perceive. See chüeh².
n^4	見	to see, to perceive, to notice, to be impressed by.
n^1	親	nearly related; affection, liking for; one's own, one's self.

chien 見		184 yen 言

chü¹	覷	to spy, to peep, to look slily.
chüeh²	覺	to perceive, to be sensible of, to feel. See *chiao⁴*.
kuan¹	觀	to look, to observe; to manifest; external appearance; many; Taoist temple.
kuei¹	規	compasses; rule, custom, usage; to rule, to regulate; to plan, to scheme to calculate.
lan³	覽	to look at, to observe, to inspect.
mi⁴	覓	to seek for, to search, to enquire after.
shih⁴	視	to look, to view, to behold, to regard, to examine; to receive; to behave; to lead; to teach.
tu³	覩	to look, to see, to observe, to behold, to view.

148
chiao 角

chi¹	觭	horns, antlers.
chiao¹	角	a horn; a quarter; a corner. See *chüeh²*.
chieh³	解	to extricate, to unloose, to liberate, to open; to explain.
ch'in¹	觔	tendons, muscles; inclination; a catty.
chüeh²	角	a horn; a corner; a quarter. See *chiao¹*.
ch'uo⁴	觸	to gore, to thrust, to hit against; to excite; to offend.

149
yen 言

an⁴	諳	skilled in, fully acquainted with, a thorough knowledge of.
cha⁴	詐	false, deceitful, fraudulent.

ch'a¹	譖	to put in one's word, to intermeddle.
ch'an³	諂	to flatter, to servilely praise; flattery, adulation.
chao⁴	詔	to declare, to proclaim; a proclamation.
chên¹	診	to examine, to look at; to verify; to feel the pulse.
chêng⁴	証	to bear witness to, to prove, to verify.
chêng⁴	證	to witness, to confront, to substantiate.
ch'êng²	誠	true, honest, sincere; truth, sincerity.
chi¹	譏	to ridicule, to satirize; to slander.
chi⁴	記	to remember, to recollect; to know; to record.
chi⁴	計	to reckon, to calculate; to plan, to devise; a stratagem.
ch'i³	訖	to finish, finished, ended, done.
chiang³	講	to speak to, to discourse; to explain; explanation.
ch'iao⁴	誚	to blame, to censure; to ridicule, to satirize.
chieh⁴	誡	orders, injunctions; to enjoin, to command; the commandments.
chien⁴	諫	to remonstrate, to reprove, to censure.
ch'ien¹	謙	respectful, yielding, humble; humility; quiet.
chih⁴	誌	to remember; to record; historical records.
chin³	謹	care and attention, respect, veneration, awe.
ching³	警	to command; to excite attention, to rouse.
ch'ing³	請	to request, to invite, to solicit, to ask with courtesy.

ch'ou²	讐	to wrangle, to fight; to hate; hatred; an enemy; retribution.
chüeh²	訣	a keepsake, parting words.
chu¹	誅	to put to death, to kill, to destroy, to exterminate.
chu¹	諸	many; all, the whole of, every.
chu⁴	註	to make notes, to explain; a commentary; a definition.
chun²¹	諄	to explain, to inculcate, to impress upon, to instil into.
fang³	訪	to enquire, to search for or out; to deliberate.
fei³	誹	to calumniate, to backbite, to slander, to libel.
fêng³	諷	to recite, to rehearse, to chaunt; recitative.
fu⁴	訃	an anouncement of death to friends, &c., a death-letter.
'hu⁴	護	to assist, to guard, to protect, to save, to preserve.
'hua⁴	話	language, speech, conversation.
'huang³	謊	to tell lies, lying, falsehood, lies.
'hui⁴	誨	to advise, to admonish, to instruct, to induce.
'hui⁴	諱	to shun, to avoid; to dread.
'hung⁴	誑	to cheat, to deceive, to beguile, to persuade.
hsiang²	詳	explicitness, clearness, minuteness; to report.
hsieh⁴	謝	to thank, to be thankful or grateful for; to decline.
hsü³	許	to allow, to permit; to promise; much, many.
hsüan¹	諠	uproar of many voices, clamorous, noisy; false.

hsün⁴	詢	to enquire, to investigate; to contrive, to scheme.
hsün⁴	訊	to interrogate, to examine judicially.
hsün⁴	訓	to instruct, to teach; to exhort, to persuade; instruction.
i²	誼	a friend; a disinterested friend; virtue, goodness.
i²	詣	to go to, to arrive at; to, at.
i⁴	譯	to translate; a translator, an interpreter. See yi⁴.
i⁴	議	to discuss, to consult, to deliberate; to plan; to select.
jang⁴	讓	complaisant, polite, yielding; to yield; to give place to.
jên⁴	認	to recognise, to know, to be acquainted with, to acknowledge.
kai¹	該	to owe; ought, should; right, proper.
k'ai³	諧	to speak; to agree; harmony, peace.
kao⁴	誥	to command, to proclaim, to enjoin; a declaration.
k'o⁴	課	to examine; to attempt; to plan; to counsel; to tax; a task.
k'ua¹	誇	to boast, to brag, boasting.
k'uang¹	誆	to lie, to deceive, to cheat.
k'uang³	誑	lies, falsehood; levity of speech; incoherence.
kuei³	詭	to reprimand, to blame; to deceive; to insult, to villify; strange, odd.
liang⁴	諒	to believe; to confide in, to trust; to suppose; to know; to assist; to oversee.
lün⁴	論	to discuss, to discourse about, to consult, to reason.
lun⁴	論	same.

mi²	謎	a riddle, a puzzle, an enigma; to puzzle.
mo²	謨	well organized plans; plans fully matured and settled.
mou²	謀	to plan, to plot, to devise; to consult, to deliberate; a plan, a stratagem.
niu⁴	謬	perverse, contrary, mistaken, erroneous, fallacious.
no⁴	諾	to answer, to assent, to promise; yes, approbation.
o²	訛	mistaken, erroneous, false, untrue; to move, to excite.
pang⁴	謗	to backbite, to villify, to slander.
p'i⁴	譬	to compare; for instance; to suppose, for the purpose of illustration.
pien⁴	變	a change, an alteration; to change, to alter; insurrection.
p'ien³	諞	to boast, to brag; specious, plausible, artful, imposing.
p'in⁴	聘	to speak; speech; to invite.
p'ing²	評	to discuss, to deliberate; to criticise; to fix, to arrange.
p'u³	譜	a register; a treatise; a biography; a genealogical table; a tune; a list; a certificate; to arrange.
su⁴	訴	to tell, to inform, to state, to accuse; calumny, detraction.
sung⁴	訟	to tell, to report; strife, contention, wrangling, litigation.
sung⁴	誦	to recite, to chaunt; a recitative; to discuss, to dispute; to calumniate.
shan⁴	訕	to backbite, to slander, to villify, to libel.
shan⁴	諂	to instigate, to seduce to, to impose upon.
shê⁴	設	to place, to arrange, to establish, to institute; to suppose; a band of soldiers; large.
shih¹	詩	poetry, verse, an ode.

shih⁴	試	to try, to endeavour, to experiment; to examine; to compare; to use, to employ.
shih⁴	誓	an oath; to swear, to vow, to bind solemnly; commanded, appointed.
shih⁴	識	to recognise, to know, to distinguish.
shih⁴	諡	an epitaph, an eulogy; posthumous titles.
shui²	誰	who? whose? what?
shuo¹	説	to speak, to say, to converse, to narrate, to explain, to teach; to scold; words, speech.
tan⁴	誕	a birthday; incoherent, to talk at random; to lie; great, wide.
t'an²	談	to chat, to gossip, to converse, chit-chat; to dispute.
t'ao³	討	to demand, to exact; to cause; to direct; to investigate; to excite; to kill; to put away.
t'êng²	謄	to copy, to transcribe; a copy-book.
t'iao²	調	to mix, to blend, to stir up; the air or tune.
ting⁴	訂	to criticise, to examine; to compare; to deliberate; to adjust, to settle; to edit.
t'o¹	託	to commission, to entrust; to engage to do; to lean upon.
tu²	讀	to read, to study; to excite; a comma, a colon.
ts'an²	讒	to backbite, to slander, to calumniate; to criticise.
ts'an⁴	譖	mutual anger; to spy, to watch.
tz'ŭ¹	詞	tales, stories; language, speech; to speak; to accuse; a term, a phrase.
wei⁴	謂	to speak of; to style or call; to say, to tell; to send; to trust.
wu¹	誣	to lie, to deceive; to accuse falsely; calumny, slander.
wu⁴	誤	to leave undone, to fail in doing, to neglect; deceitful, false, erroneous; to deceive.

ya⁴	訝	to be startled, to express surprise, to think strange.
yang¹	䛵	knowledge, wisdom; to know; to tell.
yao²	謠	lies, falsehood, slander; rumour; to slander; a ballad.
yeh⁴	謁	to state to, to declare; to request, to petition; to visit a superior.
yen²	言	words, talk, discourse; to speak, to express.
yen⁴	諺	a proverb, a common saying, tradition.
yi⁴	譯	to translate; a translator, an interpreter. See i⁴.
yü²	諛	to flatter; flattery, adulation.
yü³	語	language, sayings, words, speech, phrases, expressions; to tell, to state.
yü⁴	諭	edicts, orders; to proclaim; to interrogate.
yü⁴	譽	to praise, to speak highly of; reputation.
yü⁴	誘	to induce, to seduce, to mislead, to entice, to tempt; to teach; to advise.

150
ku 谷

'huo¹	豁	enlarged, liberal; to open, to expand.
ku³	谷	a valley, bed of a stream; a bamboo spout; to nourish; the east wind.

151
tou 豆

ch'i³	豈	how?
chiang¹	豇	beans, pulse.

*fêng*¹	豐	rich, affluent; abundant, flourishing.
*shu*⁴	豎	upright, perpendicular; to establish; chaste; a eunuch.
*tou*⁴	豆	pulse.
*yen*⁴	豔	fresh, bright; good; handsome; luxurious; dissipated.

152
shih 豕

ʻ*hao*²	豪	brave, heroic, martial, warlike; a porcupine.
*hsiang*⁴	象	the elephant.
*shih*³	豕	the hog; bristles.

153
chai 豸

*chʻai*²	豺	the wolf.
ʻ*huan*¹	獾	the badger, the fat of which is used for burns, scalds, &c.
*mao*¹	貓	the cat.
*mao*⁴	貌	air, manner, figure, countenance, personal appearance.
*pao*⁴	豹	the leopard.
*tiao*¹	貂	the marten or sable.

154
pei 貝

*chang*⁴	賬	an account, a bill.
*chên*¹	貞	virtuous, chaste, pure, uncorrupted.

chên⁴	賑	to relieve, to give, to bestow, in charity.
chien⁴	賤	mean, low; cheap, of little value.
chih²	質	to substantiate, to pledge; to examine; an agreement.
chu⁴	貯	to accumulate, to store up, to hoard; a hoard.
chuan⁴	賺	to earn money by trade, &c.; to undersell; to hinder.
chui⁴	贅	repetition, tautology; to connect.
êrh⁴	貳	two, both. Same as 二.
fan⁴	販	to traffic, to deal in; a dealer, a hawker, a pedlar.
fei⁴	費	expense, expenditure; use of, waste of; profuse, liberal.
fu⁴	負	to bear on the back; to turn the back on; ingratitude; to fail; to owe.
fu⁴	賦	to exact; exactions, tribute; to receive; to diffuse; a poem.
'ho⁴	賀	to congratulate; congratulations; to receive, to sustain, to bear.
'hui⁴	賄	a bribe; to bribe; riches, opulence.
'huo⁴	貨	goods, commodities, merchandize; to deal, to sell; to bribe.
hsien²	賢	virtuous, moral, worthy; a term of respect.
i²	貽	to leave or be left to, to bequeath.
i²	貤	to transfer rank to one's father or ancestors.
kou⁴	購	to seek; to buy.
ku³	買	to buy; to sell; a dealer, a merchant; a shop.
kuan⁴	貫	to string, to connect, to involve, to implicate.

kuei⁴	貴	dear, valuable; honourable, high, lofty, noble; to desire; important.
kung⁴	貢	tribute; merit; to offer up to.
lai⁴	賚	to give, to confer, to bestow.
lai⁴	賴	to lean on; to trust to, to depend on; to assume what is not true.
lin⁴	賃	to rent a house; to pay for the loan of anything.
lu⁴	賂	to bribe; a means or opportunity of doing.
mai³	買	to buy, to purchase.
mai⁴	賣	to sell.
mao⁴	貿	to deal, to trade, to barter, to buy or sell.
pei⁴	貝	pearls; valuable, precious; a duke; tortoise shell.
p'ei²	賠	to restore, to make up a deficiency or loss.
pên¹	賁	rage, anger; ardent, impetuous.
pien³	貶	to cast off; to censure, to dispraise, to detract; to injure.
pin¹	賓	a guest, a visitor, a stranger; to submit.
p'in²	貧	poor, poverty.
sai⁴	賽	to rival, to compete with, to contend for; to recompense.
shang³	賞	to confer, to bestow, to grant, to reward; to praise, to commend.
shê¹	賒	to credit, to give credit, to trust; to owe; distant.
shêng⁴	賸	remainder, overplus; to increase; to assist.
shu²	贖	to ransom, to redeem, to reclaim, to atone for.

tai⁴	貸	to borrow; to lend; to confer upon, to give; to forgive.
t'an¹	貪	to covet, to desire; covetous, avaricious.
t'ieh¹	貼	to stick to, to paste against, to attach to; to lose.
tu³	賭	to play, to gamble, to bet, to risk.
ts'ai²	財	riches, wealth, property, valuables, goods.
tsan⁴	贊	to counsel, to assist; to enter; to praise; to give.
tsan⁴	讚	same.
tsang¹	贓	bribes; booty, spoils, unjust gain, stolen goods.
tsê²	責	responsible for; to reprove, to reprimand, to chastise; to ask; to require; a fault.
tsei²	賊	robbers, rebels, any malefactors; to rob, to plunder; to maltreat.
tsêng⁴	贈	to present, to confer, to bestow.
tzŭ¹	資	goods, commodities, necessary things; to help.
tz'ŭ⁴	賜	to present, to confer upon, to bestow.
ying²	贏	to win, to conquer, to overcome, to succeed.
yüan²	員	any civil or military officers; round; to circulate.

155

ch'ih 赤

ch'ih⁴	赤	carnation, flesh color; naked.
'ho⁴	赫	bright, fiery; a great reputation.
shê⁴	赦	to forgive, to remit, to release, forgiveness, pardon.

156
tsou 走

ch'ao¹	超	to step over; to excel, to surpass, to precede.
ch'ên⁴	趁	to embrace an opportunity, to avail one's self of.
ch'ên⁴	趂	same.
ch'i³	起	to get up; to commence; the commencement, the origin.
ch'ieh¹	起	slanting, sloping.
ch'ü¹	趨	to walk, to go, to run after; to aspire to.
ch'ü⁴	趣	pleasure, gratification, enjoyment, relish.
fu⁴	赴	to go to, to hasten to.
kan³	趕	to pursue, to run after, to endeavour to overtake.
lieh⁴	趔	to slip, to stumble.
shan⁴	趲	to jump, to leap, to skip; to go slowly.
tsan³	趲	anxious to go; to advance, to step forward; to urge, to press upon.
tsou³	走	to walk, to go, to run.
yüeh⁴	越	to exceed, to pass over, to overstep; more; to scatter.

157
tsu 足

chi¹	跡	a footprint, a trace, a track.

chi¹	躋	to ascend, to rise, to climb.
chi²	蹟	to bequeath; bequeathed; old (as old rt coins, tales, &c.)
ch'iang³	蹌	quick; to step quickly; to fence, fencing.
chiao¹	跤	bones of the leg.
ch'iao¹	蹺	to raise the feet, to nurse the leg.
chien⁴	踐	to tread or trample upon.
ch'ou²	躊	irresolute, undecided, wavering.
chüeh⁴	蹶	to jump, to leap; to stumble; a horse's hoof
ch'u²	蹰	undecided, irresolute, embarrassed.
ch'u²	躇	to hop, to skip; irregular, undecided.
ch'uai³	踹	to limp, to waddle.
ch'uai⁴	踹	to beat or stamp with the foot; the heel.
'huai²	踝	the ankle; alone, single.
jou²	蹂	to tread, to stamp; misfortune, calamity.
k'ên¹	跟	the heel; to follow; to accompany.
k'ua⁴	跨	to bestride; to pass over, to surpass; to sit with one leg hanging.
kuei⁴	跪	to kneel.
lu⁴	路	a road, a track, a path, a passage, a way.
p'a²	跁	to climb; to creep, to crawl, to crouch, to gr
.p'a²	趴	same.

p'an²	蹣	to sit cross-legged, to squat.
p'ao³	跑	to run, to run away, to race; to evacuate.
sa¹	趿	slip-shod, down at heel, trailing.
t'i²	蹄	a hoof; to kick.
t'i⁴	踢	to kick.
t'iao⁴	跳	to jump off the ground, to leap, to skip; to walk; to overpass.
tieh¹	跌	to stumble, to slip, to fall down. See tsai¹.
to⁴	跺	to stamp the foot.
tun¹	蹲	collected together; conchant; to squat.
tun³	躉	a whole number, wholesale, by the lot.
tsai¹	跌	to tumble; to stamp. See tieh¹.
ts'ai³	踩	to stamp; the heel.
tsao⁴	躁	impetuous; haste, precipitate; to disturb, to agitate.
ts'êng⁴	蹭	confused, embarrassed; dilatory.
tsu²	足	the foot; enough, sufficient, full, complete; to complete.
tsung¹	踪	a footstep, a trace; to tread in the footsteps of.
tsung¹	蹤	same.
tz'ŭ³	跐	to tread upon, to put the foot upon. 踏.
wo⁴	踒	to sprain.

158
shên 身

ch'ü¹	軀	the human body.
kung¹	躬	the body; one's self, one's own person.
shên¹	身	the body; trunk of a tree; hull of a ship; I, one's self.
tan¹	躭	to loiter, to delay; excessive indulgence.
t'ang³	躺	to lie down, to recline.
to⁴	躲	to avoid, to withdraw, to hide, to conceal; the body.

159
ch'ê 車

chê²	轍	a track, the rut of a wheel, a footprint.
ch'ê¹	車	a carriage, cart or wheelbarrow.
ch'ên³	輾	to turn (as a wheel); to turn half round.
chi⁴	輯	to unite, to join together; to compose.
chiao⁴	較	to compare; to wrangle, to argue.
chiao⁴	轎	a sedan chair.
ch'ing¹	輕	light; to esteem light, to treat lightly; levity.
chou²	軸	an axletree; a roller for a picture.
chün¹	軍	an army, 12,500 men.
chuai³	輈	to bump or jolt, as a cart on an uneven road.

chuan¹	轉	to turn round or about, to revolve; to transport.
fu³	輔	to help, to assist.
'hui¹	輝	brightness, splendour, dazzling.
'hung¹	轟	roar of thunder, cannon, &c., roar, rattle, rumbling.
hsia²	轄	to regulate, to govern.
hsüan¹	軒	a handsome cart; a pleasant comfortable room.
juan³	輭	soft, flexible, yielding, delicate, weak.
juan³	軟	same.
ku¹	軲	a carriage.
ku³	轂	the nave of a wheel, an axletree; a wheel; a carriage.
liang⁴	輛	a pair of wheels; a cart; Numerative of carts.
lün²	輪	a wheel; large, great; north and south. See lun².
lu²	轆	a sort of windlass to draw water; a block, a pulley.
lun²	輪	a wheel; large, great; north and south. See lün².
nien³	輦	the imperial chariot; near the Emperor or court.
pei⁴	輩	a generation; a sort, a class, a series, a company.
p'ei⁴	轡	reins.
shu¹	輸	to lose; to ruin; to exhaust; to offer to, to present to.
t'ang³	輎	a time, a turn; an axle; a ruled line.
tsai³	載	to contain; to fill; to effect; to record; then; year; cycle; laden; many.

ts'ou⁴	辏	near; to collect together, to assemble, to accumulate.
ya⁴	軋	crunching of wheels; a punishment.

160

hsin 辛

hsin¹	辛	acrid, bitter; grievous.
ku¹	辜	fault, crime, guilt; to oppose; a necessity imposed.
la⁴	辣	sharp, pungent, acrid, hot.
pan⁴	辦	to administer, to manage, to transact, to do; to provide, to prepare.
pan⁴	辯	to dispute, to quarrel; to debate, to insinuate. See pien⁴.
pien⁴	辨	to cut asunder, to divide; to distinguish; to dispute, to discuss; to ascertain.
pien⁴	辯	to discriminate, to judge; to insinuate; specious; to dispute, to debate, to quarrel. See pan⁴.
pien⁴	辮	the pigtail, the Chinese queue; to plait.
tz'ŭ²	辭	to decline, to refuse; to separate from, to leave; to speak; language; an expression.

161

ch'ên 辰

ch'ên²	辰	a period of time (the Chinese hour); 7 to 9 o'clock a.m.
ju⁴	辱	to insult, to shame, to disgrace, to defile, to debauch.
nung²	農	a countryman; to cultivate, to plant, to sow.

162
ch'o 辵

chê¹	遮	to cover over, to screen, to conceal; to stop.
chê⁴	這	this person or thing. See chei⁴.
chei⁴	這	this, this one. See chê⁴.
ch'êng⁴	逞	presumptuous, forward, precipitate.
chi¹	迹	a footprint, a trace, a track. See 跡.
ch'i³	迄	to reach to, to extend to; finally, at last. See hsi³.
ch'ien¹	遷	to ascend; to move to, to remove, to shift, to alter.
ch'ien³	遣	to send, to commission.
ch'ih²	遲	to delay, slow, dilatory, late.
chin⁴	近	near (either in time or place), recently.
chin⁴	進	to enter; to ascend; to make progress.
ching⁴	逕	a bye-road, a footpath, a short cut, direct; the diameter. Same as 徑.
ch'iu²	逑	to join, to unite.
chou¹	週	to revolve, to circulate, to turn round.
chu²	逐	to expel, to drive away; to attend to each in turn.
chui¹	追	to escort, to follow after, to pursue.
êrh³	邇	near to, close to, at hand.
fan³	返	to return, to revert to, to come back.

fêng²	逢	to meet; to occur; to oppose.
'hai²	還	still, even now, yet, also. See 'huan².
'huan²	還	to return, to repay. See 'hai².
'huang¹	遑	unoccupied, disengaged, at leisure; pressed, urged.
'hui²	迴	to turn round, to return.
hsi³	迄	to reach to, to extend to, to, till; finally, at last. See ch'i³.
hsiao¹	逍	to saunter, to stroll for pleasure.
hsüan³	選	to choose, to select.
hsün²	巡	to cruise, to go the rounds, to patrol, to make a tour of inspection.
hsün⁴	迅	speedy, sudden, quick, hasty, expeditious.
hsün⁴	遜	humble, respectful, complaisant, retiring, yielding.
i²	遺	to leave, to bequeath; to lose; a will, a bequest.
i²	迤	the side, the border.
i²	逸	ease, leisure, idle; to lose; to abscond; to set free.
jao⁴	遶	to go about or around, to surround.
kuang⁴	逛	to walk for pleasure, to stroll.
kuo⁴	過	to pass, to exceed; past; perfect tense; error, fault, crime.
la²	邋	slovenly, dirty, untidy.
liao²	遼	remote, distant, far off.
lien²	連	to connect, to unite, to join; to return to; in succession; and, even, also.

lin²	遴	to walk or act with difficulty; stingy; to desire, to covet; to select carefully.
liu²	遛	to linger or lurk about.
lo²	邏	to cruise, to patrol; a patrol; to surround; to screen.
mai⁴	邁	to go, to walk; to pass, to exceed; to disregard; aged.
mi²	迷	to puzzle, to stupify; stupid, deceived; perturbed; to lose; to stray off.
nai³	迺	in, at, is, am, was, but, doubtless, certainly, forsooth; your; and. See 乃.
ni⁴	逆	disobedient, rebellious, contrary to, opposed to; confusion.
pêng⁴	迸	to jump off the ground; to saunter, to rove; to walk apart; to cause or send.
pi¹	逼	to press, to constrain, to urge, to compel; to tyrannize over.
pi⁴	避	to avoid, to shun, to withdraw, to retire from.
pien¹	邊	the side, the border, the frontier, the edge.
pien⁴	遍	everywhere, all round or through; to pervade; a time or turn. Same as 徧.
po⁴	迫	extreme, urgent, pressing; to embarrass.
su²	速	quick, fleet, haste, hurried, promptly, instantly.
su⁴	述	to relate, to narrate; to state to; to rehearse; to publish; to continue. See shu⁴.
sui²	遂	to accompany, to follow; to succeed; to advance; next, then, after that, forthwith.
sung⁴	送	to send to, to carry to; to present; to accompany.
shih⁴	逝	to depart, to return to; to die.
shih⁴	適	just now; presently; suddenly; certainly; to go to; to arrive at; to occur.
shu⁴	述	to relate, to narrate; to state to; to rehearse; to publish; to continue. See su⁴.

ta²	達	intelligent; to know; to inform; passing through; successful; to promote; all, every.
t'a⁴	躂	to spoil, to injure; a hurried, hasty step.
tao⁴	道	a road, way or thoroughfare; to speak, to say; reason, principle.
t'ao⁴	逃	to run away, to abscond, to escape.
ti⁴	遞	to give or hand to; to change, to alter; for, in place of, instead of.
tieh²	佚	satisfactorily; change, alteration; ease, indulgence.
tou⁴	逗	to stop, to delay, to remain; to dwell; to tempt.
t'ou⁴	透	to penetrate thoroughly; to discern, to comprehend; to exceed.
t'u²	途	a road, way or path (physically and morally).
t'ui³	退	to retire, to withdraw; to drive back; to decline, to refuse; to return.
tun⁴	遁	to skulk off, to run away; concealed; to hide one's self.
t'ung¹	通	to understand, to perceive clearly; to pass through; all; complete; to succeed; prosperous.
tsao¹	遭	to meet, to encounter, to occur, to happen; a time or turn; to injure, to spoil.
tsao⁴	造	to make, to do, to act, to build, to commence; to receive; to advance.
tsun¹	遵	to obey, to yield, to submit, to follow; obedience; to accord with.
wei²	違	to oppose; to delay; to relinquish, to vacate; perverse, wicked.
yao¹	邀	to invite, to request, to want.
yao²	遙	remote, distant, far.
ying²	迎	to meet, to welcome, to receive; to occur.
yü⁴	逾	to exceed, to overpass; still more; remote, distant.

yü⁴	遇	to meet; to happen, to occur, to fall in with.
yüan³	遠	remote, distant (in time or place).
yün⁴	運	to transport, to convey; to move, to agitate; to circulate; to bring to pass.
yu²	遊	to roam, to wander, to stroll; to flow, to float, to swim.

163
i 邑

chiao¹	郊	waste land outside a city; the country.
chün⁴	郡	a district; a populous place.
hsiang¹	鄉	a village; the country; a province; 12,500 families.
hsieh²	邪	deflected, bad, vicious, depraved, obscene, lewd.
i⁴	邑	a town, a city.
kuo¹	郭	a waste, a common; suburbs.
lang²	郎	a complimentary term applied to persons.
lin²	鄰	near to, connected with, neighbours; five families; assistants; ministers.
na³	那	what? how? where?
na⁴	那	that. See na³.
pang¹	邦	a country, a state, a nation.
pi⁴	鄙	vulgar, coarse, rustic; low, mean, vicious, bad; to despise, to condemn; not; nothing.
pu⁴	部	tribe, class, genus; list, category; a public court; division of a book.
tu¹	都	all, the whole [number, general; the capital; to dwell.

| ts'un¹ | 邨 | a village, a hamlet. |
| yen⁴ | 艶 | fresh, bright, good, handsome, luxurious; dissipated. |

164
yu 酉

chiang⁴	醬	a kind of pickle made from pulse, &c.; soy.
chiao⁴.	醮	to burn incense; to pray; a widow marrying again.
chiu³	酒	wine, spirits, any kind of fermented liquor.
cho²	酌	to pour out wine; to consult, to deliberate.
ch'ou²	酬	to return the compliment, to give an equivalent.
ch'ou³	醜	ugly, deformed; hateful, offensive; to detest, to abhor.
ch'un²	醇	attention, respectful; wine; essence; semen. See *shun²*.
'han¹	酣	half-intoxicated, elevated, cheerful, merry, jolly.
hsing³	醒	to awaken, to be roused.
i¹	醫	to heal, to cure; to treat; a doctor; the medical profession.
lao⁴	酪	cream; a liquor made from mare's milk.
lei⁴	酹	to pour wine upon the ground in sacrifice.
niang⁴	釀	to excite, to ferment.
p'ei⁴	配	to mate, to match with; a pair; to pair; an equal, a fellow, an associate.
su¹	酥	a preparation of butter and flour.
suan¹	酸	sour; grieved, afflicted; debilitated.

*shai*¹	釃	to warm (as wine); to purify; to separate, to divide.
*shun*²	醇	wine, cordial; thick liquids; respectful; attentive, observant. See *ch'un*².
*ts'u*³	醋	vinegar.
*tsui*⁴	醉	drunk, intoxicated.
*yen*¹	醃	pickle, brine; to preserve in brine.
*yu*³	酉	wine; 5 to 7 P.M.; evening; finished, completed.

165
ts'ai 釆

*shih*⁴	釋	to release, to free, to disperse, to dissipate, to melt; to explain; to happen; Buddhism.
*ts'ai*³	釆	bright colours, elegant, brilliant.

166
li 里

*chung*⁴	重	heavy; important; severe; to repeat; repeated; in duplicate.
*li*²	釐	to subject, to regulate, to govern; copper coin (cash); twins; a pair.
*li*³	里	Chinese mile (⅓ of English); a lane; a village.
*liang*²	量	a measure; to measure; to calculate; the capacity; feelings; views; a limit; to judge.
*yeh*³	野	the country, moor, common, wilderness, rustic, wild.

167
chin 金

*ch'ai*¹	釵	a large pin, a bodkin.

ch'ao⁴	鈔	government money orders or notes.
chên¹	針	a needle.
chên¹	鍼	same.
chên⁴	鎮	to keep down, to repress, to rule; a town.
ch'iang¹	鎗	a lance, a spear; a musket; firearms in general.
chiao³	铰	a spade or shovel; a hinge; a hoe; scissors.
ch'iao¹	鍬	a shovel or spade; a hoe.
chien¹	鐫	to engrave, to carve; a style or chisel.
chien¹	毽	a shuttlecock.
chien³	鐗	a kind of mace; the iron of an axle-tree.
chien³	鋄	to gild, to wash with silver or gold.
chien⁴	鑒	a mirror; to reflect light; a precept.
chien⁴	鑑	same.
ch'ien¹	鉛	lead, blacklead.
ch'ien²	錢	copper coin; money, wealth; 1/10th of a tael, a mace.
ch'ien³	鉗	forceps, nippers, pincers, tweezers, tongs; to nip, to pinch; earrings.
chin¹	金	gold; any metal.
chin³	錦	figured or flowered silk.
ching⁴	鏡	a looking-glass, a mirror.
cho²	鐲	bracelets.

chü⁴	鋸	a saw; to saw.
chüeh³	钁	a hoe.
chün⁴	鈞	30 catties, one fourth of a picul; large.
chu⁴	鑄	to pour melted metal into a mould, to cast.
ch'u²	鋤	a hoe.
ch'uan⁴	釧	an armlet, a bracelet.
chui¹	錐	an awl; a point; a trifle.
ch'ui²	鎚	a mallet, a hammer; to beat, to strike.
ch'ui²	錘	a weight; heavy; a hammer.
chung¹	鍾	a cup; to like.
chung¹	鐘	a bell; a clock; certain tones in music.
ch'ung⁴	銃	a small cannon, a gingal.
fêng¹	鋒	the point of a weapon; the van of an army.
fu³	釜	a cooking-pan.
hsi²	錫	tin; to confer, to bestow; to receive.
'hsiang¹	鑲	a border; to border, to inlay.
hsiao¹	銷	to expend; to dissipate, to melt; to destroy; expended.
hsien¹	銑	a shovel or spade; to burnish.
hsien²	銜	a bit or bridoon; to control; brevet rank.
hsiu⁴	銹	rust.

*jui*⁴	銳	a pointed weapon; sharp, keen, piercing.
*kang*¹	鋼	steel.
*k'o*⁴	錁	small silver ingots.
*kou*¹	鈎	a hook; a sickle; a spear; to hook; to d to drag; to induce.
*k'ou*⁴	釦	to ornament or inlay with gold, &c.; a but
*kuo*¹	鍋	a cooking-pan.
*liao*³	鐐	fetters, irons; silver; fine white metal.
*lien*²	鏈	a chain; connected; locked together; or
*lien*²	鎌	a hook, a sickle.
*lien*⁴	鍊	to melt metals; to refine, to purify; ma expert in; to practise.
*ling*²	鈴	a small bell; empty words.
*lo*²	鑼	a gong.
*lu*⁴	錄	to transcribe, to record; a record, a narr a list or index; order, series; to take.
*luan*²	鑾	an imperial carriage; bells.
*man*⁴	鏝	a trowel.
*mao*²	錨	an anchor.
*ming*²	銘	to engrave; to write; to publish; to reco
*nao*²	鐃	cymbals.
*nieh*⁴	鑷	tweezers, nippers, forceps, tongs, snuffers.
*niu*³	鈕	a button; a knob.

pa⁴	鈸	a small bell; cymbals.
pên¹	錛	an adze.
p'iao⁴	鏢	a shaft; a weapon; point of a knife, &c.
po¹	鉢	a sacrificial vessel,
p'u⁴	鋪	a shop; to spread, to arrange, to extend.
so³	鎖	a lock; to lock, to fetter; rings; a chain.
tang¹	鐺	the sound of a drum.
tei¹	鏑	the point of an arrow; tweezers.
têng⁴	鐙	stirrup irons.
tiao⁴	釣	a hook; to hook, to fish, to take.
t'ieh³	鐵	iron.
tien⁴	鈿	golden flowers or ornaments for a lady's head-dress.
ting¹	釘	a nail, a pin, a bolt; to nail.
ting⁴	錠	an ingot of silver (value about 10 taels.)
tu⁴	鍍	to gild, to wash with silver or gold.
tun⁴	鈍	blunt, dull, stupid.
t'ung²	銅	copper, brass.
tsan⁴	鏨	a small chisel; to carve, to chisel.
ts'ê¹	鍘	a knife for chopping up straw, &c.
tso²	鑿	a chisel; to dig; to open; to mark; to make, to do.

ts'o⁴	錯	to err, to mistake, wrong, erroneous; mixed; confused; strange, perverse.
tsuan¹	鑽	to bore, to pierce, to worm one's self into; to, search out; a gimlet, an auger.
yao⁴	鑰	a key; a lock; a bolt.
yin²	銀	silver; money.
yüeh⁴	鉞	an axe or hatchet.

168
chang 長

chang³	長	to grow; to extend. See ch'ang⁴.
ch'ang⁴	長	long, length; senior. See chang³.
ssŭ⁴	肆	four; noisy, riotous; profligate, dissolute; error; excess; extreme; great, large; to arrange.

169
mên 門

cha²	閘	a gate, a pass, a canal lock.
chien¹	間	a space or interval; to diminish; to separate; Num. of rooms, &c.
ch'üeh¹	闕	empty; deficient; disrespectful; a gate.
ch'uang³	闖	to rush suddenly out or in; precipitately.
'ho²	闔	a door; to shut, to cover; all; a whole family.
hsien²	閒	leisure, unoccupied, idle, loitering; empty.
hsien²	閑	to defend, to guard against; without occupation, leisure.

jun⁴	閏	an intercalary month.
k'ai¹	開	to open, to unfold, to unloose; to begin; to boil.
ko²	閣	an upper room; a council chamber.
kuan¹	關	to shut, to bar, to bolt; to concern; a bolt.
kuei¹	閨	private apartments of ladies.
k'un³	閫	a door-post; the gates of heaven; ladies' apartments.
k'uo⁴	闊	open; wide, broad; remote, distant; long apart; perverse; painful.
mên²	門	a gate, an entrance, a door; a class; a profession.
min²	閩	a kind of snake; official name of Fuchien.
pi⁴	閉	to close, to shut, to screen, to conceal; to store; to stop up.
shan³	閃	a flash; instantaneously, momentarily; to shun, to evade; to peep.
wei²	闈	to surround, to besiege; to guard; to limit.
wên²	聞	to hear; to smell; to state to.
yen¹	閹	testicles; a eunuch; to castrate.
yüeh⁴	閱	to look at, to survey, to review, to inspect, to examine; to read.

170

fu 阜

a¹	阿	affirmative particle. See o¹.
a³	阿	interrogative particle; final sound.

chên⁴	陣	to arrange or form in ranks; the army; a gust; a shower.
ch'ên²	陳	to state to; a long time, old, stale.
chi⁴	際	time, period, juncture, crisis, opportunity.
chiang⁴	降	to descend; to condescend; to cause to submit. See hsiang².
chieh¹	階	stairs, steps; a step, a degree in rank.
chieh⁴	隔	to separate; separated, apart from. See ko².
chih¹	隲	to attain; to succeed.
ch'u²	除	to exclude, to deduct, to subtract, to put away; to except from.
fang²	防	a bank; to guard, to keep off, to defend, to be prepared.
fu⁴	附	near, neighbouring to; to join; to depend on; an appendix; a supplement; an enclosure.
fu⁴	阜	a mound of earth.
hsiang²	降	to cause to submit; to yield, to submit, to obey. See chiang⁴.
hsien³	險	danger, dangerous; difficult.
hsien⁴	陷	to fall into; to descend, to sink, to involve; to ruin. See hsüan⁴.
hsien⁴	限	limit, limited.
hsüan⁴	陷	to fall into, to descend, to sink; to involve; to ruin. See hsien⁴.
ko²	隔	separated, apart from. See chieh⁴.
ling²	陵	the imperial tombs; high, eminent; to aspire; to insult; to invade.
liu⁴	陸	six. See lu⁴. Same as 六.
lou⁴	陋	ugly; low, mean, petty, obscure; a dirty alley; uninformed.

lu⁴	陸	six ; dry land ; in succession. See liu⁴.
lung²	隆	Imperial ; high, eminent, conspicuous, glorious ; rich ; abundant.
lung³	壟	a bank, a dike, a ridge.
o¹	阿	an exclamation. See a¹.
pei¹	陂	uneven, not level.
p'ei²	陪	to bear company, to second, to assist, to attach to ; to benefit ; to fill up.
pi⁴	陛	steps ; steps leading to the Imperial throne ; the sides.
sui²	隨	to yield ; following after ; according to ; forthwith, immediately.
shan³	陝	name of a province.
shêng¹	陞	to rise, to ascend ; to go up steps ; to advance ; to be promoted.
t'ao²	陶	a furnace ; earthenware ; to melt ; to transform.
ti¹	隄	an embankment, a shore ; a limit, a fence ; a bridge.
t'o²	陀	steep ; a Buddhist syllable.
tou³	陡	sudden ; to stop, to desist ; steep.
tui⁴	隊	an army, a group, a company.
ts'u⁴	阻	to hinder, to prevent ; to stop ; to suspect ; to be sorry.
yang²	陽	the male principle ; light and heat ; the sun ; openly.
yin¹	陰	shady, obscure, sombre, dark, dull ; female ; inferior ; the moon.
yin³	隱	dull, gloomy ; hidden, secret ; to avoid, to conceal ; to pity.
yüan⁴	院	a court, palace, mansion, college, temple or hospital ; a court-yard ; an enclosure.

171

tai 隶

*li*⁴   隶   attendants in public offices; to be attached to.

172

chui 隹

*chi*¹   雞   the fowl.

*ch'iao*³   雀   a sparrow; any small birds.

*chih*¹   隻   single, alone; one of a pair; Numeral of ships, &c.

*ch'u*²   雛   the young of any birds.

*hsiung*²   雄   male, masculine; martial, brave, heroic; a hero.

*ku*⁴   雇   to hire; to obtain labour for money.

*li*²   離   to leave; to separate; from; distant from or to; to divide into pairs; in order, arranged.

*nan*²   難   difficult; difficulty, distress, suffering, grief; grievous, hard.

*sui*¹   雖   though, although, supposing or admitting it to be.

*shuang*¹   雙   a pair, a brace; double.

*tiao*¹   雕   to carve wood, to grave.

*tsa*²   雜   mixed, blended; miscellaneous; confused; extremely; a privy.

*tz'ŭ*²   雌   female of birds.

*ya*³   雅   elegant, refined, learned; pure, simple; correct, decorous.

yen⁴　雁　the wild goose. Same as 鴈.

yung¹　雍　to assist; to collect together; to crowd; harmony.

173
yü 雨

chên⁴　震　to shake, to agitate; a shock.

hsia²　霞　a halo, vapour, a red sky, variegated clouds.

hsiao¹　霄　vapour, clouds; sleet; a halo; heaven; infinite space.

hsü¹　需　to use, to employ.

hsüeh³　雪　snow; to whiten; to clear one's self; to revenge.

lei²　雷　thunder; a loud noise; to echo, to reiterate.

li⁴　霖　noise of thunder.

lin²　霖　abundant or genial rain.

ling²　零　small rain; the residue; fractional; odd numbers; a cipher.

ling²　靈　spiritual, subtile, ethereal; intelligent; efficacious; the soul.

lou⁴　露　to disclose, to divulge, to discover, to make apparent. See lu⁴.

lu⁴　露　dew. See lou⁴.

pa⁴　霸　to domineer; to usurp, to incroach upon; an usurper.

pao²　雹　hail.

p'i¹　霹　the shock and noise of thunder, earthquake, &c.

sha⁴　霎　fine rain, a slight shower.

shuang¹	霜	frost, hoar-frost; cold, frigid, grave; a crystallization.
tien⁴	電	lightning.
wu⁴	霧	mist, fog, vapour.
yü³	雨	rain; to rain.
yün²	雲	clouds; vapour, fog.

174
ch'ing 青

ching⁴	靜	sky coloured; azure; green; pale, wan.
ch'ing⁴	青	silence, stillness, calm, quiet, repose.
tien⁴	靛	indigo.

175
fei 非

fei¹	非	not, wrong, false; low, vicious.
k'ao⁴	靠	to lean against, to depend on, to trust to.
mi²	靡	to scatter; extravagant, wasteful; selfish; destitute of, not having, not being.

176
mien 面

mien⁴	面	the face, the surface; the front; towards; the first appearance of things.

177
ko 革

an¹	鞍	a saddle.
ch'an⁴	韂	saddle flaps.
ch'iao⁴	鞘	a sheath, a scabbard.
ch'ien¹	韆	a swing; to swing.
ch'iu¹	鞦	the harness of a horse, mule, &c.
hsieh²	鞋	shoes, slippers.
hsüeh¹	靴	boots.
ko²	革	to flay; to degrade, to reject; hide.
lung²	韁	a bridle.
pien¹	鞭	a whip, a lash, a rod; to whip, to flog.
wa⁴	韈	stockings.

178
wei 韋

t'ao¹	韜	a quiver or sheath, a scabbard; wide, broad.
wei²	韋	dressed leather.

179
chiu 韭

chiu³	韭	leeks, scallions.

180
yin 音

hsiang³	響	sound, noise, clamour, music; a signal, a call.
yin¹	音	sound, tone, notes; news, intimation of.
yün⁴	韻	air, tune; to rhyme; last syllable of a line; final sound.

181
yeh 頁

ch'an⁴	顫	to tremble with cold; to smell.
chia³	頰	the jaws.
ch'ing³	頃	a hundred *mu*; cautious, careful; a moment, an instant.
ch'üan²	顴	the cheek bones.
'han¹	頇	slow, tardy, dawdling, dilatory.
hsiang⁴	項	the neck; kind, sort; item, thing.
hsien³	顯	apparent, visible, conspicuous; to manifest.
hsing⁴	顖	the top or crown of the head.
hsü¹	須	requisite, necessary, must; to expect.
kêng³	頸	the neck.
k'o¹	顆	a bead; Numerative of beads, grain, &c.
k'o¹	頦	to lower part of the face, the chin.

ku¹	顧	to look over the shoulder, to look; a protecting look; to lead.
lei⁴	類	class, species, kind, sort, category, genus.
ling⁴	領	a collar; the neck; to govern, to put in order; to direct; to receive.
lu²	顱	the head, the skull, the forehead.
man¹	顢	dawdling; a large face; effrontery.
o²	額	the forehead; a fixed number; incessant.
pan²	頒	to send away, to disperse, to disseminate, to spread; to confer.
p'o¹	頗	very, extremely; rather; doubt, suspicion; uneven, deflected.
sai¹	顋	the jaws, the side of the face.
sang³	顙	the front; the middle of the forehead.
sung⁴	頌	to praise, to extol.
shun⁴	順	obedient; accompanying; prosperous; to obey, to comply, to suit, to yield; harmonising.
t'i²	題	a theme, a subject, a proposition; to praise; to write poetry; the head, the forehead.
tien¹	顛	to upset, to turn over; the top, the head, the forehead; to amble.
ting³	頂	crown of the head; the top, the summit; knob or button worn by mandarins.
t'ou²	頭	the head, the top, the chief; the front; the sides; the end.
tun⁴	頓	a time, a turn; a meal; to bow the head; to part with; sudden.
wan²	頑	thick-headed, obstinate; foolish, silly, stupid. Same as 玩.
yeh⁴	頁	the head; the leaf of a book, &c.
yen²	顔	the countenance; colour.

yü⁴	預	beforehand, previously arranged, prepared, provided against; easy; cheerful.
yüan⁴	願	to wish, to desire; to be willing; each, every; a vow.

182
fêng 風

fêng¹	風	the wind; usage, custom.
ʻhu¹	颳	a stiff breeze, a gale.
hsüan⁴	颴	a whirlwind.
kua¹	颳	to blow; a strong wind.
pʻiao¹	飄	to whirl round; a whirlwind; to be blown; to fall; easy flowing gait.
sou¹	颼	sound of the wind.
yang²	颺	to let off, to escape punishment; to sail off; to fly away; to winnow.
yao²	颻	whirling round.

183
fei 飛

fei¹	飛	to fly, to flee, to go quickly.

184
shih 食

chan¹	饞	greedy, gluttonous.
chi¹	饑	scarcity, dearth, famine, want, hunger.
chiao³	餃	a mince pie.
chien⁴	餞	to salt rice; a farewell banquet or meal; to present.

shih 食		shih 食

ch'ih⁴	飭	to enjoin, to command; to adjust; compact, firm.
chin³	饉	a scarcity of vegetables, a dearth.
chüan³	餶	a kind of pancake.
chuan⁴	饌	food, provisions, victuals.
êrh³	餌	a kind of cake, a meat pie.
fan⁴	飯	boiled rice, food in general; a meal.
'hu²	餬	gruel; food, sustenance, subsistence; to subsist.
'hun²	餛	a kind of small meat pudding.
hsiang³	餉	soldiers' pay or rations; duties, taxes.
hsiang³	饗	a sacrifice; to sacrifice; to entertain, to banquet.
hsien⁴	餡	fruit, meat, &c., put into pastry; stuffing of any kind.
hsiu¹	饈	dainty viands; to nourish, to feed.
jao²	饒	overplus, excess; to spare, to excuse, to forgive.
kao¹	餻	a kind of steamed pudding; a bait; gruel.
kuan³	館	tea or eating-house; an inn, a hall, a school, an establishment.
k'uei⁴	饋	food, victuals; to prepare food; to present to, to offer in sacrifice.
k'uei⁴	餽	a sacrifice; presents of food; to leave to.
man²	饅	cakes, bread, a dumpling.
nang³	饢	to eat; to force to eat; to eat with a keen appetite.
o⁴	餓	hungry; hunger, famine. = 飢

pao³	飽	to eat to fullness, satiated; indolent.
ping³	餅	a cake, cakes, pastry.
po¹	餑	cakes.
san³	饊	rice boiled till it separates.
sou¹	餿	rotten rice, rice spoiled by damp and heat.
shih¹	飾	to adorn, to paint, to brighten; to wipe, to cleanse, to gloss over; ornaments; weapons.
shih²	食	to eat; to drink; to feed; food.
ssŭ⁴	飼	to feed.
t'ien³	餂	to lick; to touch; to hook.
t'un⁴	飩	a kind of cake.
ts'an¹	飧	an evening meal; dressed food.
ts'an²	餐	to eat.
wei⁴	餧	to feed animals.
yang³	養	to rear, to bring up, to support, to nourish, to feed.
yao²	餚	prepared food, provisions, victuals.
yin³	飲	to drink; to rinse the mouth.
yü²	餘	surplus, overplus, remainder; to spare.

185
shou 首

shou³	首	the head, chief, first, foremost; beginning or origin of; a leader; to lead; to show.

186
hsiang 香

fu⁴	馥	fragrant, fragrance.
hsiang¹	香	fragrant, fragrance, incense, scent.

187
ma 馬

ch'i²	騎	to ride any animal astride.
chia⁴	駕	an imperial carriage, a cart; a term of respect.
chiao¹	驕	proud, haughty, arrogant, ungovernable.
ch'ih²	馳	to gallop, to ride on horseback.
ching¹	驚	to startle, to alarm, to affright, to astonish.
chü¹	駒	a colt, a young horse.
ch'ü¹	驅	to gallop; to lash or flog a horse.
chün⁴	駿	a fine looking horse.
chu⁴	駐	to halt and rest; an encampment, cantonments, a garrison; to garrison.
'huan¹	驩	the frisking or playing of a horse; fresh.
hsiao¹	驍	bold, enterprising, daring.
hsieh²	駭	alarmed, startled, terrified. Also 'hai.
i⁴	驛	post; to post; post horses; government express; a stage. See yi⁴.
k'o⁴	騍	a mare.

| *ma* 馬 | | 226 | *ku* 骨 |

lo²	騾	a mule.
lo⁴	駱	the camel.
lü²	驢	the donkey.
ma³	馬	the horse; enraged; martial.
p'ien⁴	騙	to defraud, to swindle; to leap on horseback.
po²	駁	to contradict, contradictory; diverse; freckled; to remove.
sao¹	騷	to stir, to fidget; disturbed, fidgety, agitated; mournful; lame.
shih³	駛	haste, hurry, fleet, to hasten, to run fast, to sail fast.
t'êng²	騰	to ascend, to rise; to lift; to transfer; to propagate; to run; to leap upon.
to⁴	馱	a beast's load.
t'o²	駝	the camel; to load on a beast's back; to carry.
ts'ao³	騲	female of domestic animals.
tsung¹	騣	a mane.
yen⁴	驗	to inspect, to examine; to witness, to verify; proof, testimony.
yi⁴	驛	post; post horses; government despatch. See *i⁴*.

188
ku 骨

ang¹	骯	dirty.
ku³	骨	a bone, bones.
k'u¹	骷	a skeleton; the shoulder-blade.

lou²	髏	the skull.
pang³	髈	the shoulders; the hips, the thighs.
sui³	髓	marrow.
shai³	骰	dice.
t'i³	體	a body, the human body; real, substantial; decent; to give effect to; to realize.
tsang¹	髒	dirty; fat; bony; large-bodied.

189
kao 高

kao¹	高	high, lofty, eminent, elevated.

190
piao 髟

chua¹	髽	mode of braiding a girl's hair; a woman's hair when in deep mourning.
fa³	髮	the hair of the head.
fang³	髣	like, resembling, similar, seeming as if.
fu²	髴	the hair in disorder; like, resembling, seeming as if.
'hu²	鬍	the beard, the whiskers.
'huan²	鬟	a female slave or servant.
hsü²	鬚	the moustache.
jan²	髯	the beard, the hair of the face.
kuan¹	鬠	tonsure of a Taoist priest.

lan¹	鬣	a horse's mane; long hair.
pin⁴	鬢	the hair on the temples, the temples.
pin⁴	鬂	same.
sung¹	鬆	loose, easy, slack, lax, dishevelled; to loosen.
tsung¹	鬃	a mane.

191
tou 鬥

chiu¹	鬮	a lottery, a kind of ballot.
chiu¹	鬪	same.
'hung⁴	鬨	to squabble, to quarrel; to excite; to fight.
nao⁴	鬧	bustle, noise, confusion, tumult, uproar; to be in a rage; to scold.
tou⁴	鬥	to fight.
tou⁴	鬭	to fight, to contest, to wrangle; to meet, to occur.

192
ch'ang 鬯

yü⁴	鬱	melancholy, vexation, anxiety.

193
ko 鬲

None.

194
kuei 鬼

ʻhun²	魂	shade, manes, spirit, ghost or soul.
kuei³	鬼	a ghost, spirit, demon or devil.
kʻuei²	魁	great, eminent; the head, headmost.
mo²	魔	a spirit, demon or devil.
pʻo⁴	魄	a spirit, the spirit, the animal soul; form, figure.
wei⁴	魏	high, lofty, elevated.

195
yü 魚

chi³	鯽	the name of a small fish, the bream.
chiao¹	鮫	a kind of dog-fish or shark.
chʻiu¹	鰌	a kind of eel.
ʻhuang²	鰉	the sturgeon.
hsia¹	鰕	crabs, prawns, shrimps, lobsters.
hsien¹	鮮	live or fresh fish; fresh, bright, clean, pure.
kuan¹	鰥	an old bachelor; a widower.
li³	鯉	the carp.
lin²	鱗	the scales of fishes.
lu³	魯	stupid, dull, blunt; mixed, confused; Shantung.

yü 魚	230	*niao* 鳥

pao⁴ 鮑 stinking fish; a surname.
piao⁴ 鰾 glue.
shan⁴ 鱓 the eel.
yü² 魚 fish of any kind.

196
niao 鳥

chi¹ 鶏 the fowl. See 雞.
ch'iao³ 鵲 the magpie.
chiu¹ 鳩 a pigeon or dove; to assemble; to rest.
chüan¹ 鵑 a kind of cuckoo.
ch'un¹ 鶉 a kind of quail.
fêng⁴ 鳳 the phœnix.
fu² 鳧 wild ducks.
'hao² 鶴 a kind of stork.
'hung² 鴻 a large kind of wild goose; a stork; great, vast.
k'o¹ 鴿 the pigeon or dove.
kua¹ 鴰 the rook.
kuan⁴ 鸛 the crane.
li² 鸝 the mango bird.
lu⁴ 鷺 a kind of pelican, a heron.

luan²	鸞	a fabulous bird.
niao³	鳥	a bird, birds generally.
o²	鵝	the goose.
p'êng²	鵬	a fabulous bird, the roc.
ssŭ¹	鷥	a sort of pelican used for catching fish.
tiao¹	鵰	a hawk, a buzzard; to carve.
wu³	鵡	a species of parrot.
ya¹	鴉	the crow with a white breast.
ya¹	鴨	the duck.
yang¹	鴦	female of the mandarin duck.
yen⁴	鴈	the wild goose. See 雁.
ying¹	鷹	a falcon, eagle or hawk.
ying¹	鶯	a kind of thrush.
ying¹	鸚	a parrot.
yüan¹	鴛	the male mandarin duck.

197
lu 鹵

chien³	鹼	a kind of salt, soda.
hsien²	鹹	salt taste, salted, preserved in brine.

lu³	鹵	salt, natural salt.
yen²	鹽	salt, salted, to salt.

198

lu 鹿

chang¹	麖	the musk deer.
li⁴	麗	elegant, graceful, beautiful, good, fair, flowery, bright.
lin²	麟	a large stag (fabulous); splendour, light.
lu⁴	鹿	the deer.
p'ao²	麃	a kind of deer.
shê⁴	麝	the musk deer.
ts'u¹	麤	large, coarse, rough, vulgar; remiss; sandals.

199

mai 麥

ch'ü²	麯	a ferment for making spirits.
fu¹	麩	bran.
mai⁴	麥	wheat.
mien⁴	麵	wheaten flour.
mien⁴	麪	same.

200
ma 麻

'hui¹ 麾 a colour or standard; to signalize.

ma¹ 麼 interrogative particle. See mo¹.

ma² 麻 hemp; numb, numbness.

mo¹ 麽 interrogative particle. See ma¹.

201
'huang 黃

'huang² 黃 yellow.

202
shu 黍

li² 黎 black hair; many, numerous; all, daybreak.

nien² 黏 paste; to paste; to be connected with; to make to adhere.

shu³ 黍 millet.

203
'hei 黑

'hei¹ 黑 black, dark, sombre, obscure, night.

mo⁴ 默 silent, silently, still; dark; thoughtfully.

tai⁴ 黛 painted eyebrows; to paint the eyebrows.

'hei 黑	234	shu 鼠

tang³ 黨 a gang or band; associates, companions; to involve; a place; a time.

tien³ 點 a point, a particle, a dot, a spot; to punctuate; to blot, to soil; to light; to nod.

204
chih 黹

fu³ 黼 embroidered, figured, flowered.

黻 embroidered, figured, flowered; to embroider.

205
min 黽

min² 黽 the frog; to use effort, energy.

pieh¹ 鼈 a species of tortoise, the turtle.

206
ting 鼎

ting³ 鼎 a tripod; stable, firm, correct, steady; to set up, to establish.

207
ku 鼓

ku³ 鼓 a drum; a measure; a star; a state.

208
shu 鼠

shu³ 鼠 rats, mice, squirrels.

209
pi 鼻

'hou¹ 齁 to snore; very, extremely.
nang⁴ 齉 a stoppage of the nose.
pi² 鼻 the nose.

210
ch'i 齊

chai¹ 齋 abstinence; to respect.
ch'i² 齊 even, regular, correct, complete; to adj

211
ch'ih 齒

ch'ih³ 齒 the teeth; one's age.
ch'u² 齣 a piece, a section; Num. of theatri formances.
ling² 齡 the teeth (denoting the age); the year of age.
tzŭ¹ 齜 to shew the teeth; irregular teeth.
yao³ 齩 to bite, to knaw. See 咬.

212
lung 龍

k'an² 龕 a niche, a small room; a pagoda.
lung² 龍 the dragon; Imperial.

213
kuei 龜

kuei¹ 龜 the tortoise.

214
yo 龠

None.

RADICALS.

—   入

1 STROKE.

1. *yi*   一 one; unity.
2. *kun*   丨 a stroke connecting the top with the bottom.
3. *chu*   丶 a point; a period.
4. *p'ieh*   丿 a line running obliquely to the left.
5. *yi*   乙 a character in the time cycle of China.
6. *chüeh*   亅 a hooked end.

2 STROKES.

7. *êrh*   二 two.
8. *t'ou*   亠 above.
9. *jên*   人 亻 man.
10. *jên*   儿 man.
11. *ju*   入 in, into; to enter.

2 STROKES.

12. *pa*	八	eight.
13. *chiung*	冂	border waste-land.
14. *mi.*	冖	to cover over.
15. *ping*	冫	an icicle.
16. *chi*	几	a stool.
17. *k'an*	凵	able to contain.
18. *tao*	刀 刂	a knife; a sword.
19. *li*	力	strength.
20. *pao*	勹	to wrap round.
21. *pi*	匕	a spoon or scoop; a weapon.
22. *fang*	匚	a chest.
23. *hsi.*	匸	able to contain or conceal.
24. *shih*	十	ten.
25. *pu*	卜	to divine.
26. *chieh*	卩 㔾	a joint.
27. *'han*	厂	a ledge that shelters.
28. *ssŭ; mou*	厶	private; selfish.
29. *yu*	又	again.

3 STROKES.

30. k'ou   口 the mouth.
31. wei   囗 able to enclose.
32. t'u   土 earth.
33. shih   士 a scholar.
34. chih   夂 to step onwards.
35. ts'ui   夊 to step slowly.
36. hsi   夕 evening.
37. ta   大 great.
38. nü   女 a female.
39. tzŭ   子 a son.
40. mien   宀 roof of a cave.
41. ts'un   寸 an inch.
42. hsiao   小 little.
43. wang   尢 尣 兀 bent as an ailing leg.
44. shih   尸 a corpse.
45. ch'ê   屮 sprouting; vegetation.
46. shan   山 a hill.
47. ch'uan   巛 巜 川 streams.

3 STROKES.

48.	kung	工	labour.
49.	chi	己	self.
50.	chin	巾	a napkin; head-gear.
51.	kan	干	a shield; to concern.
52.	yao	幺	small.
53.	yen	广	roof of a house.
54.	yin	廴	continued motion.
55.	kung	廾	the hands folded as in salutation.
56.	yi	弋	to shoot with the bow.
57.	kung	弓	a bow.
58.	ch'i	彐 互 彑	pointed like a pig's head.
59.	shan	彡	streaky, like hair.
60.	ch'ih	彳	to step short.

4 STROKES.

61.	hsin	心 忄 ⺗	heart, mind.
62.	ko	戈	a lance, spear.
63.	'hu	戶	a house door.

4 STROKES.

hou	手 扌	the hand.
hih	支	a prop; to issue money.
'u	攴 攵	to tap lightly.
ën	文	stripes; ornament; literature.
ru	斗	Chinese bushel.
'in	斤	Chinese pound; an axe.
ing	方	square.
'u	无 旡	not.
h	日	the sun; the day.
üeh	曰	to speak.
üeh	月	the moon.
ru	木	wood; trees.
t'ien	欠	to owe; to be wanting in.
'ih	止	to stop (neuter).
ti	歹 歺	bad.
ru	殳	a quarter-staff.
u; kuan	毋	do not!
	比	to compare; lay side by side.

4 STROKES.

82. mao	毛		hair, fur.
83. ch'i	气		vapour.
84. shih	氏		family from past time till now.
85. shui	水 氵冰		water.
86. 'huo	火 灬		fire.
87. chao.	爪 爫		claws.
88. fu	父		father.
89. yao	爻		cross-wise.
90. ch'iang	爿		the radical 91 reversed.
91. p'ien	片		a slab of wood; a slice or piece.
92. ya	牙		the back teeth.
93. niu	牛 牜		oxen, kine.
94. ch'üan	犬 犭		the dog.

5 STROKES.

95. yüan	玄	black.
96. yü	玉 王	precious stones.
97. kua	瓜	the gourd.

5 STROKES.

98. *wa* 瓦 tiles.
99. *kan* 甘 sweet.
100. *shêng* 生 to live; to produce.
101. *yung* 用 to use.
102. *t'ien* 田 fields; arable land.
103. *p'i* 疋 the bale or piece of cloth, silk, &c.
104. *ni* 疒 disease.
105. *po* 癶 back of back.
106. *pai; po* 白 white.
107. *p'i* 皮 skin; bark.
108. *min* 皿 covered dishes.
109. *mu* 目 the eye.
110. *mou* 矛 a long lance.
111. *shih* 矢 arrows.
112. *shih* 石 stone.
113. *ch'i; shih* 示 spiritual power; revelation.
114. *jou* 禸 the print of a fox's foot.
115. *'ho* 禾 any kind of grain.

5 STROKES.

116. *hsüeh*	穴	a cave.
117. *li*	立	to stand up or still.

6 STROKES.

118. *chu*	竹	the bamboo.
119. *mi*	米	rice uncooked.
120. *mi; ssŭ*	糸	raw silk as spun by the worm.
121. *fou*	缶	earthenware.
122. *wang*	网 皿 冂 冗 冈	a fishing-net.
123. *yang*	羊	sheep.
124. *yü*	羽	feathers.
125. *lao*	老	old.
126. *êrh*	而	and; but yet.
127. *lei*	耒	the plough.
128. *êrh*	耳	the ear.
129. *yü*	聿	a pencil.
130. *jou*	肉 月	flesh, meat.
131. *ch'ên*	臣	servant of the sovereign.

6 STROKES.

132. *tzŭ* 自 self, from.
133. *chih* 至 to come, or go to; arrive at.
134. *chiu* 臼 a stone mortar.
135. *shê* 舌 the tongue.
136. *ch'uan* 舛 at issue; in error.
137. *chou* 舟 ships, boats.
138. *kên* 艮 limitation; character in the time cycle.
139. *sê; shai* 色 colour.
140. *ts'ao* 艸 艹 plants; herbs.
141. *'hu* 虍 the tiger's streaks.
142. *ch'ung; 'hui* 虫 reptiles having feet.
143. *hsieh; hsüeh* 血 blood.
144. *'hang; hsing* 行 *'hang*, a row as of buildings; *hsing*, to go, to do.
145. *yi* 衣 clothes.
146. *sha; hsi* 襾 西 to cover; the west.

7 STROKES.

147. *chien* 見 to perceive, with the eye, nose, ear, or mind.

7 STROKES.

148. *chiao*	角	horns; a corner.
149. *yen*	言	words.
150. *ku*	谷	a valley.
151. *tou*	豆	beans.
152. *shih.*	豕	the pig.
153. *chai; ti*	豸	reptiles without feet.
154. *pei*	貝	the tortoise; his shell; hence, precious.
155. *ch'ih*	赤	flesh colour.
156. *tsou*	走	to walk or run.
157. *tsu*	足	the foot; enough.
158. *shên*	身	the body.
159. *ch'ê; chü*	車	vehicles; sedans.
160. *hsin*	辛	bitter.
161. *ch'ên*	辰	horary period, from 7 to 9 A.M.; a cycle character.
162. *ch'o*	辵 辶	moving and pausing.
163. *yi*	邑 阝	any centre of population.
164. *yu*	酉	horary period, 5 to 7 P.M.; a cycle character.
165. *ts'ai; pien*	釆	to part and distinguish.

7 STROKES.

166. *li*   里 a hamlet; the Chinese mile.

8 STROKES.

167. *chin*   金 the metals; gold.
168. *chang; ch'ang*   長 to grow; length.
169. *mên*   門 a gate, a door.
170. *fu*   阜 阝 a mound of earth.
171. *li; tai*   隶 to reach to, to arrive at.
172. *chui*   隹 short-tailed birds.
173. *yü*   雨 rain.
174. *ch'ing*   青 sky-blue.
175. *fei*   非 negative; wrong.
176. *mien*   面 靣 the face; the outside.

9 STROKES.

177. *kê; ko*   革 a hide stripped of hair; to strip the hide, to flay.
178. *wei*   韋 tanned hide.
179. *chiu*   韭 leeks.

9 STROKES.

180. yin 音 sound.
181. yeh 頁 the head; page of a book.
182. fung 風 wind.
183. fei 飛 to fly as birds.
184. shih 食 to eat.
185. shou 首 the head.
186. hsiang 香 fragrance.

10 STROKES.

187. ma 馬 the horse.
188. ku 骨 bones.
189. kao 高 high.
190. piao 髟 shaggy.
191. tou 鬥 to fight; to emulate.
192. ch'ang 鬯 a sacrificial bowl; luxurious vegetation; contentment.
193. ko; li 鬲 a sacrificial vase on crooked feet.
194. kwei 鬼 spirits of the dead.

11 STROKES.

i	魚	fish.
ao	鳥	birds.
	鹵	natural salts.
	鹿	the deer species.
ai	麥	wheat.
a	麻	hemp.

12 STROKES.

uang	黃	yellow; clay colour.
u	黍	millet.
ei; 'hĕ	黑	black.
ih	黹	embroidery.

13 STROKES.

êng; min	黽	of the frog or toad kind.
ng	鼎	a two eared tripod used in sacrifice.
u	鼓	the drum, &c.
iu	鼠	the rat kind.

14 STROKES.

209. *pi* 鼻 the nose.
210. *ch'i* 齊 arranged, in order.

15 STROKES.

211. *ch'ih* 齒 front teeth.

16 STROKES.

212. *lung* 龍 the dragon tribe.
213. *kuei* 龜 the tortoise, turtle, &c.

17 STROKES.

214. *yo* 龠 flutes, pipes, &c.